If you want to read about

being a kid now, not what life will be like later,

then this book is for you.

What's in this book

What's This About Being a Kid?

Maybe you've heard people say that all grownups were kids once. The people who say this are usually grownups. And they're right. In order to become a grownup, you have to be a kid first. That's a fact.

The Getting-Ready Theory of Life

Maybe you've noticed that some of the grownups in your life act like being a kid is mostly about getting ready to be an adult. People who think that way believe that your kidhood is a time for *getting ready*. Kindergarten is getting ready for first grade. Elementary school is getting ready for high school. High school is getting ready for college. And college? Well, that's getting ready for being out of college and getting a job.

Maybe all that sounds a little crazy. If now is the time for getting ready for what's coming, when do you get to enjoy *now*?

Later Comes Anyway

This is a book about being a kid now, not preparing for later. Later is going to come no matter what. (Peter Pan and his pals are the only known example of a somewhat successful try at holding back later.)

This book says that there are some things about your life that you control and there are some things about your life that you don't control. That's mostly when grownups take over and decide things for you and about you. This book won't change that. But it can help you take a sharp look at how your life is shaped just because you are a kid, along with some clues about what you might do about that.

This book says that if you explore being a kid now in as many ways as you possibly can, you'll be ready for later anyway.

The touching story of a kid who waited for later

Chapter 1

The Big Fuss

Because you are a kid, you are a very special person. Most grownups think that, and they are constantly making quite a fuss over you. You know some of these grownups real well. They're the ones who tell you to eat your broccoli, or to put on a warm jacket if you're serious about going outside, or send you just what you've been hoping for on your birthday, or help you figure out a tough long division problem. Mostly everything they do for you is for one of two reasons: to protect you from something or to teach you something. (More about these *somethings* later.)

The reason they give you all this attention is because they care about you. A lot! Even if it doesn't seem like it at times.

Then there are grownups who are constantly making a fuss over you, and you don't even know them. Or them you. And maybe you never will. Yet what they do also has a big effect on your life. They're the ones who decide that you can't go to see a certain movie unless a parent is with you, or that you can't drive a car yet, or that you have to go to school, or that there shouldn't be certain things on TV because you shouldn't see them. Mostly everything they do is for the same two reasons: to protect you or to teach you.

Why All the Fuss?

How come grownups are always doing so much for kids? In the first place, grownups are the ones who are responsible for you being in this world. And they were all kids themselves once. Really.

Even though the world was a lot different when they were kids, one thing was the same. Grownups were always doing stuff for them, protecting them, or teaching them. So now that they are grownups, they're doing what they have learned grownups do for kids.

This is not bad. Or necessarily good. It just is. Besides, adults know that kids are very important.

The Fuss Has Snags

Does all this sound suspiciously simple? Well, there are some snags that grownups get into.

One snag: There are times when grownups try to protect or teach you, and you don't think you need any of either. Then at least one of you is upset.

Another snag: There are times when grownups don't agree with other grownups about what it is you need to be protected from, or taught, or how to do it.

Still another snag: When grownups realize that they've hit snag number one or two, they don't always know what to do about it, and a disagreement can go on for a while. A long while, sometimes.

And there you are, right in the middle of snags.

Maybe you're thinking that if they get into a snag over you, how come they aren't asking you what you would like to be protected from or what you would like to learn?

If you weren't thinking that, try thinking it now.

Maybe they never thought to ask you. Maybe they don't think you are the one who knows best about your protection or learning. Maybe they are so busy discussing you with each other, they don't have time to stop and ask you.

And did you ever try to get someone's attention when they are doing something else and are very excited? It's not easy.

What This Book Can Do for You

This book can give you information about things in your everyday life that affect you — whether or not you know it. Most of these things are controlled by grownups. There isn't any way you can avoid that. And grownups are often mighty useful.

You'll get information about different topics. About laws that give you certain rights and restrictions. About how these laws dribble into your life at home and at school. About money in your life. About work. About television and movies. About kids that are mistreated.

About talking to grownups with and without words.

But what's most important is that you'll explore how you really feel about these topics and how they affect you. You'll learn when you might be able to do something about them in your life. This can help you when you get stuck in one of those snags.

A Reminder About Your Kidhood

Remember, you may be special because you are a kid, but it is not a kid's world. Why else would they put telephones so high in booths, for example?

But being a kid in a grown-up world shouldn't mean that you are a short grownup-in-training. It means you have to deal with grownups a lot. Every day. The better you can do this, the better you can get on with being a kid.

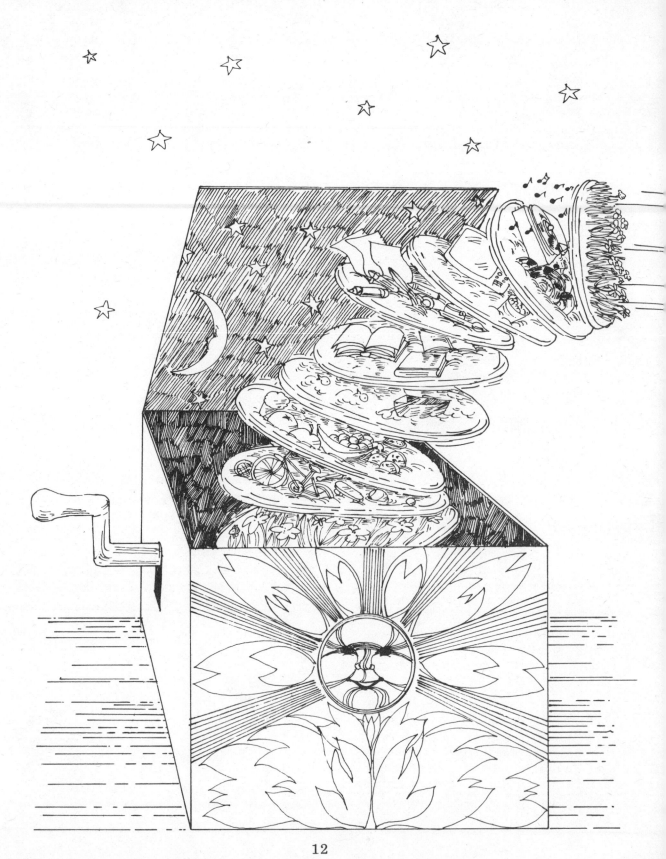

Chapter 2

What Kind of a Kid Are You, Anyway?

Do you know what kind of kid you are? Most likely, you've got something to say about that. But you can never know too much about yourself. When you're reading this book, you will be getting a lot of information about the grown-up world you live in, and how grownups have shaped your life. It's important that you do more than just let the information slide past your eyes into your brain. Stop and investigate how you feel about the information — how it shapes your life, and what you might want to do about it.

To get you warmed up, here are some activities to get you started thinking about you.

The Who-Am-I ? Game

You need some equipment for this activity: a friend, a way of timing one minute, paper, and a pencil. You and your friend should sit facing each other, at a table or cross-legged on the floor. Your friend has two jobs. One is to ask you, "Who are you?" The other job is to do this over and over again until one minute is up. What you do is to answer each time with a different idea. Don't write anything yet.

Here's a sample:

Who are you? A daughter
Who are you? A sister
Who are you? A football fan
Who are you? A Ping-Pong player
Who are you? A kind person
Who are you? A messy person

Try it. When the minute is up, write down as many of the things you can remember you answered. When you've finished your list, ask your friend to look it over to see if there are things you left out.

Now switch roles so your friend can make his or her list. A hint: A minute can seem like a long time when you are the person being asked the question over and over. That's part of the activity. It helps you to think of things about yourself you might not think of first off. Don't stop the game, accusing your friend of forgetting to watch the clock. Stay with it and keep searching for different ways to describe yourself.

When you've got your lists, here are some more ideas to help you look at yourself in new ways:

1. Add any other things you think belong on the list but that you never said. Help each other add to your lists.

2. Sort the list into three kinds of responses. Put an A next to those things that describe who you are in relation to other people (daughter, sister). Put a B next to those things that describe what you do (Ping-Pong player, football fan). Put a C next to those things that describe qualities you have (kind, messy). Which group is the shortest? Can you add any to the group which has the least number of things in it? Which category is the biggest? How come?

3. One more thing you can do with your list. Use another sheet of paper. In the center of the page, write *I Am* or *Me.* And then write all the words from your list in some design around the center. Using different colored felt-tip pens or colored pencils helps to make it look really super. Hang it up in your room. That way you can remind yourself about all that you are, in case you have a sudden case of brains-in-your-shoes.

14

A Quiz with No Wrong Answers

Here's a twelve-question quiz. For each question, you answer **Yes** or **No**. There are no wrong answers. These are questions which help you to pin yourself down on what you think about different things.

(1) Do you think everyone needs to learn to read and write?

(2) Do you think everyone should have to go to school for a certain amount of time?

(3) Do you think kids your age should be allowed to vote for President of the United States?

(4) Do you think kids should get an allowance?

(5) Do you think kids should work for an allowance?

(6) Do you think it's possible to watch too much T.V.?

(7) Do you watch too much TV?

(8) Do you think kids should be allowed to see any movie they want to?

(9) Do you think older brothers and sisters should discipline younger ones?

(10) Do you think kids should decide what time they go to bed?

(11) Do you think there are times when it's OK to lie?

(12) Do you think it's important to have a best friend?

Do you think you would have answered these questions the same way three years ago? Do you think you'll feel the same way three years from now? How about at the end of next summer?

Where Does Your Time Go?

How do you spend your time? And who decides that? Think of a regular ordinary weekday. Put the four things below in this order. First comes what you think you spend the most time doing. And last is what takes the least amount of time. The other two go in order in between.

Being in school, including getting there and home.
Sleeping.
Playing, doing things you choose to do.
Doing chores or other stuff outside of school that you have to do.

Now keep a record for several regular weekdays. Make a chart like this for your record. Was your prediction accurate?

What about on weekends or holidays? How much of that time do you get to do just about what you want? Keep a chart for a weekend and see where your time really goes.

TIME CHART

Date: _Jan. 10_

Time	Activity
11 p.m. – Midnight	Sleeping
Midnight – 1 am	
1 – 2 am	
2 – 3 am	
3 – 4 am	
4 – 5 am	
5 – 6 am	
6 – 7 am	
7 – 8 am	Getting dressed, Chores
8 – 9 am	School
9 – 10 am	
10 – 11 am	
11 am – Noon	
Noon – 1 pm	
1 – 2 pm	
2 – 3 pm	
3 – 4 pm	Playing
4 – 5 pm	
5 – 6 pm	
6 – 7 pm	Supper and Homework
7 – 8 pm	- - - - -
8 – 9 pm	TV
9 – 10 pm	
10 – 11 pm	Sleeping

Total Hours :

School ___7___

Sleeping ___9___

Chores ___2½___

My own
choice ___5½___

Put a List in Your Life

This activity gives you a look at those things you like to do, things you choose to do when you get the chance. You need a piece of paper and something to write with. You can do this one alone or with someone else. It's interesting to compare your results with someone else.

Here's what you do. Number your paper from 1 to 15. Then next to each number, write something that you like to do. Big things or little things. Alone things or together things. Inside or outside. As long as they are things you just love to do when you get the chance. Stop reading now and start listing.

When you've got your list done, here are some things you can do with it:

Put a check next to the three things you like to do most. (Were these the first three you thought of?) If you asked your parents what three things you like to do most, do you think they'd pick the same three you did? Would your sister or brother know? Your best friend? Who would guess the closest? Try it and see.

Put a dollar sign ($) next to all the things you like to do that cost money. Now which of these statements fits your list most?

Everything I like to do costs money.

Most of the things I like to do cost money.

About half the things I like to do cost money.

Hardly anything I like to do costs money.

③

Put a **k** next to all the things on your list that only kids like to do. Things that grownups usually don't like to do or don't do. How many of your 15 things have a **k**?

There are other things you can investigate on your list. How about seeing if the things you like to do are inside things or outside things? Or things you do alone or with friends? Which have you not done for a while?

Suppose you decided to plan a perfect day, one where you'd just do things you love to do. There's nothing you have to do except have a perfect day. Think about a plan. Is it possible for you to really spend a day like this? Why not? Have you tried?

Putting Your Feelings in Order

This is an exercise for making up your mind that is different from deciding yes or no. It gives you more choices. You have to decide which you think is the best choice, the next best, and the next best, down to the one you like the least. There are no right or wrong answers. They are for you — to think about you. Some of them will be easier than others. See how you feel when you have a hard choice to make.

What kind of present do you most like to get for your birthday?

☆ One that is a total surprise
☆ One that you already know about
☆ One that you got to pick out

How would you spend $5 that was given to you?

☆ On something to wear
☆ On something to play with
☆ On a bunch of little things — candy, comics, stuff like that

Which would you rather be?

☆ An only child
☆ The youngest child
☆ The oldest child

Which would you like least?

☆ To move to a new school
☆ To lose the $5 that someone just gave you
☆ To break your arm

Which do you like most?

☆ To play alone
☆ To play with one good friend
☆ To play with a few friends
☆ To play with a big group of kids

Sometimes you have to make choices about how to handle a situation. This method can come in handy. First write down a question that's on your mind. Then list the possible choices and rank them. It's another way to think about you. Right now.

Confusing You with Some Facts

Even if you haven't spent a lot of time thinking about who and what you are, lots of other people have. Grownups, for the most part. Here are some facts you can try on.

There are more than 55 million people in the United States who are under the age of 15. That's a little more than one-fourth of the country's population, which is a sizable chunk. No wonder adults tend to make a bit of a fuss over you; there are too many of you to ignore.

Here's what else grownups have found out about kids. Over 95% of all kids live in families. Almost three out of every four kids live with their two natural parents. About 16% live in one-parent homes, most of them with their mothers. About 25% of all kids have parents who are not still married to the people they first married. Over 60% of kids live in cities. Under 5% live on farms. More than half of all kids' mothers work outside the home.

From a study that the United States Government sponsored, in 1972 in a town in southern California, lots of other statistics were collected about how kids spend their time. The kids in this study were all sixth graders. They watch TV for about 30 hours a week, 17 to 18 of those hours on weekdays. More than half listen to the radio for more than a hour a day. Almost three-fourths own their own radios. They don't go to the movies very often, but almost half listen to records for more than an hour a day. About one-third of the kids don't read comics at all, but one-third read five or more in a month. About one-third don't read books, but about one-fourth read more than four books each month. Three-fourths of the kids read newspapers and of those, half read the comics, and one-fourth read only the front page. Over half the girls talk on the telephone every day or at least several times a week; only one-third of the boys use the phone as often. And on and on. It can make your head spin. Which of these statistics fit you? Which don't? Could you write your own statistical autobiography?

Watch Out for Shoulds

A warning: All the activities in this chapter have nothing to do with "should." None of that "I should be like this," or "I should do things like that." That kind of thinking can only get in the way of your exploring what kind of kid you really are. Inside and out.

A 1972 survey of one town found out that....

Almost three out of every four kids live with their two natural parents.

More than half of all kids' mothers work outside the home.

Over half the girls talk on the telephone every day, or at least several times a week.

About one-third of the kids don't read comics at all, but one-third read five or more in a month.

Chapter 3

The Legal You

Here's a chance to look at yourself through binoculars, the way grownups see you. Grownups you don't even know. Laws have a lot to say about who you are as a kid and how you manage during your kidhood.

The laws were written by grownups over a long period of time, probably not by any grownups you've ever known. So here's a case where people you haven't met have a lot to say about how your life goes.

The law makes you special. That means you, everyone you know who is a kid, and all the kids you don't know. The law makes you all special in the same way. You are all kids.

There is an enormous collection of laws that people have agreed to live by. They can be enforced when someone does something that violates these laws. Grownups have generally agreed that they need to protect and to teach kids. And over a long time, they've gotten more and more specific about how they intend to do both of those things. These laws got written down so that everyone could know about them.

Do you know about them? It seems you should. They are written about you and your life.

What Do You Know About Your Rights?

Try this legal quiz. For each statement answer true or false:

1 You have the legal right to demand that your parents support and educate you.

2 You have the legal right to an education.

3 You have the legal right to dress any way you like in school so long as it doesn't get in the way of anyone's discipline or learning.

4 You have the legal right to work at any available job so long as it doesn't interfere with your schooling.

5 You have the legal right to spend or save the money you earn.

6 You have the legal right to have a bank account and to deposit and take out money without needing your parents' permission.

7 If you borrow money, you are legally responsible to repay it.

How much do you know about your legal rights? How much do your parents know about them? Ask them the questions. Maybe the whole family needs a bit of legal instruction.

It would be nice if there was a tidy list of all the laws that affect you, so you could read through them, like the rules for checkers or softball. Well, forget that. They're long, complicated, and written in a form of English that only lawyers understand. Lawyers go to school for years to learn it. (Some lawyers even begin talking in a strange way. Try asking a lawyer what you think is a simple question about the law. Watch him or her sigh before trying to translate the answer into regular English for you.)

Back to you. How does the law make you special? Legally, you are a minor. Do you know what that means? Well, keep reading. Mostly that entitles you to special protection. Protection from what? And how do you get that protection? These are the questions that are reasonable, but tough to answer. The law is rarely simple.

The Birth of the Legal Infant

Here's some history. Over 150 years ago, British common law stated why there should be minors and how they should be treated. (Common law grew from rules that people used for a long, long time. Courts made decisions using these rules, and eventually they became written, formal laws.) The idea about minors was that when infants were born, they didn't have the experience needed to protect themselves from the evils of the world. Because of this, they were entitled to some protection. And people were considered infants until they became 21. Legally, that is.

What does British common law of 150 years ago have to do with you today? A lot. Most of the laws that affect you — and grownups as well — came from British common law. The laws are called statutes and are set by the legislature in each state.

In the law today, you are a minor until you reach the age of majority. Even the word *infant* is still used to describe you. And the age of majority isn't the same for all kids since it's set by the state you live in.

There's more to it. You reach the age of majority for different things at different ages, even though you are just one person living in just one state. All kids in the United States can vote when they're 18. But you have to be 21 in lots of states in order to buy alcohol, while you may be able to get full adult driving privileges in some states as young as 15 or 16.

Some of the laws have changed over the last 150 years. There sure wasn't any need for laws about drivers' licenses then. But being a legal infant means that there are certain restrictions on you. You just can't do all that adults can, because you're not considered to have enough experience.

Chapter 4

Bringing It All Home

How parents and kids get on today isn't how it always was. There wasn't always such a fuss made over kids. Not that parents loved their children less or took care of them more poorly. Mothers have always protected, fed, and looked after their children. It was just different. Children had a much different place in the world than they do today.

From Infants to Adults

Not much is known about how kids were treated in ancient times. There are a few hints. It seems that grownups thought of kids as infants until about the age of seven. Not necessarily exactly seven, since exact birthdays weren't so important then as now. Children were no longer considered infants when they no longer needed special attention from their mothers. Then they entered adult life. That meant boys began to do what men did —

hunting for food, working on the farm, tending cattle. And girls did what women did.

After infancy came adulthood. Just like that. This was also true later in time. You can see children in old paintings from about the 1100s. They were always pictured as little adults. They were dressed as adults, and often had expressions on their faces that made them look more like adults than children, except that they were smaller.

Some reasons for this? Infants died more often than they lived. Montaigne was a French writer who lived in the 1500s. When writing about his infant children, he said, "All mine die." He sounded like an unsuccessful gardener, talking about his tomato plants. Maybe not much fuss was made as a protection against feeling bad in case a baby died. Infants were taken care of, but when they got a little older, there was no separate world for the time of childhood as there is today. Children got along as well as they could in the only world there was — the adult one.

By the 1600s, a slight difference in parents' feelings appeared. When a young child died, it was given more attention than it had been earlier. Dead children began to be represented on their parents' tombstones. In general, children weren't ignored quite so much. Grownups coddled them more. They played with them and enjoyed watching them. But there was still no separate life for children. They shared the same games with adults, the same toys, the same stories. Adults and children were always together.

After infancy, at the age of about seven, the child was expected to participate in the adult world. They didn't always stay at home and work. Often children went to live in other homes, as apprentices, to serve the head of a household.

Today it's very natural for parents to send their children off to school for most of the day. They have to. It's the law. So kids spend at least seven to nine years in school. At that time, it seemed perfectly OK for parents to send children off to be apprentices for seven to nine years. It wasn't unusual for kids to live away from home like this.

How parents and children got along was much different then. One reason is that there were no schools that seven-year-olds went to. The only schools were for training clergymen, not for the general education of all children. There were no pediatricians and no child experts to tell families what was good for their kids. There was no choice for children but to get on with being adults.

Imagine that you are a seven-year-old again. You really wouldn't need constant care from your parents anymore. And pretend that there are no schools. So now you would get to do whatever it is that grownups do with their time. No one would ever say, "Nope, you can't do that. You're just a kid." You would be expected to do whatever work needed to be done. You would have to pull your own weight, not just hang around and play all day. Can you imagine what your life would be like?

Richer people had easier lives with much less hardship. But children in these families still were not separated from adult life, and at the age of seven they too were no longer seen as infants.

26

The Story of Louis

Here's one example of the childhood of a boy named Louis. This is true. Louis was born on September 27, 1601. He was Louis XIII. His father was Henry IV, King of France at that time. So Louis was rich. His doctor kept a diary of what he did each day. This helps to tell his story:

From an early age, Louis did much the same things as adults did. He played and danced and sang with grownups. At the age of four, he danced in adult ballets.

At five, he practiced archery and played cards. He played charades at six. He liked fairy stories, but so did most grownups at that time.

He liked to play hide-and-seek, blindman's bluff, fiddle-de-dee. But adults played also.

There were some things he did before the age of seven that grownups didn't do. He played with dolls. He had a hobbyhorse he liked to ride. He had a toy windmill that he especially liked, and he zoomed around the palace with it.

Sometimes he was disciplined, like for

refusing to eat his supper. Though Louis did receive special attention for being a child, he was allowed to take part in all the adult activities. Grownups generally found him cute and amusing.

But at the age of seven, there was a change. It didn't happen overnight. Louis probably didn't notice it very much, but grownups began to encourage him to give up his childlike toys.

His infancy was seen to be over. He was taught to gamble. He began to learn to ride, shoot, and hunt, spending more time with men. The message was clear. First came infancy. Then came adulthood.

How does Louis's life seem to you?

The Invention of Childhood

This way of life for a child was not looked on as very sensible by everyone. Another attitude was held during the 1600s, mostly by religious men or monks. They felt that children were a bit more fragile and needed more protection than they had been receiving. They felt that letting them take part in all of adult life was absolutely ridiculous — that this was no way to help a child develop into a good thinking grownup and a Christian. Children shouldn't be pampered little people, coddled, played with, and then suddenly dumped into adult life. They needed some preparation. They needed strict discipline, constant supervision, special books to learn from. They needed to learn manners from an early age, and they needed to use them in everyday life. Infancy needed to stretch into childhood, so all this training could take place.

These religious teachers, mainly Jesuits, felt there was another need for education besides training clergymen. They thought that parents had more responsibility for preparing children for adult life than just passing on their name to the next generation. They had the big job of shaping their children. And the best way to shape their children was to send them to school. By sending children away to school, the children would be protected from adult life. And parents would be fulfilling the job of giving their children a good preparation for life.

Parents began to agree with the Jesuits. School was a replacement for the apprenticeship, and more and more parents sought to educate their children. They began to take a different interest in their children, and became more involved in thinking about their future. At first only boys could go to schools, but by the end of the 1600s, schools were available for girls also.

Not all children went. Poorer children didn't have the chance; they were still apprenticed to other households or worked at home. Very rich people often chose not to send their children to school. But there was definitely a change in families. Parents were becoming much more concerned about the futures of their children. They were trying to do more to protect and teach them. This meant children were separated more and more from adult life. This was an important change.

Eventually all of this trickled down to the working classes. But it took a while. In the 1800s in the United States and Europe too, the children of working-class parents still took part in most of adult life. They had no choice. They could work, and their earnings were needed to help support their families. But the change in how parents saw their responsibilities was taking hold.

At this time, children generally lived at home until they were 16 to 18 years old. This gave parents much more contact with their children and helped to change emotional ties. Besides, health care improved a great deal. Fewer kids died. Along with this extra contact came more separations between the lives of children and the world of adults. Laws were passed so that children couldn't buy tobacco or gamble. By the beginning of the 1900s most states had passed laws that made it compulsory for children to attend school. Sunday schools were organized for children. Other organizations were formed: Scouts, 4-H, YMCA, YWCA.

There used to be infancy and then adult life. Then there got to be three stages: infancy (until you were four or five), kidhood (from the end of infancy), and adulthood. No child was any longer expected to share the lives of grownups. And that's generally the way it is today.

At first there was only infancy and then adulthood.

Then that changed to three stages so there was time to be a kid too.

A Look at Your Life Line

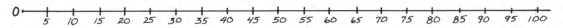

Suppose this line represents your life. That little circle at the left end is really a zero. That's how old you are when you're born. Draw a life line just like this on a piece of paper and then try these activities.

① At what age do you think you will die? Make a dot to show where you think your life will end. The average number of years that men live is 68. For women, it's 72 years. Why do you think there is a difference in men's and women's life spans?

② Divide the line into three parts. Each part will represent one of the three stages: infancy, kidhood, adulthood. Divide the line so that each stage gets a part of the line, and each part shows how much of your life you spend in that stage.

③ Now draw yourself in where you think you are now.

④ When do you think is the best time of life? Are you in it? Did you pass it already? Do you think it's yet to come? Put a hump in your line to show where your best time might be.

Some people say that life begins at 40. They might put a hump in their life line like this:

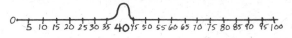

Some people say that life was best before they had to do anything, before they had to go to school. These people also say, "Too bad I didn't know then what I know now." They might put humps like this:

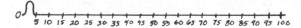

30

Barron

Two Worlds

As the lives of children and adults became more separate, kids' lives filled up with kids' things: music, books, clothes, feelings. Grownups were not a part of this. They were off busily being grownups. Kids weren't able to participate in grownups' lives. Grownups grew farther and farther from what really made up the lives of their children.

Younger children came to be more closely influenced by older children than by adults. Although the two worlds were kept separate, adults still kept control of what kids could and couldn't do. Often there was quite a stir. When rock music first started to become popular, many grownups got quite upset. They didn't understand the music, found it dreadful to listen to, and suspected it was bad for kids. Ask your parents what went on when Elvis Presley first came on TV. Kids decided that long hair was OK for boys as well as for girls. Grownups got all upset. Schools made rules. Parents and kids had conflicts at home. In the 1960s more and more kids ran away from home. They felt they wanted to live their lives much differently than their parents. They became the "flower children" and were described as hippies.

These changes have crept up on families in less than four centuries. Plus there have been many other changes in our world, changes caused by the increase in science and technology. The world has become very much more complicated. Ask your parents what was different in the world when they were kids. No wonder families have had to change — enormously. And they probably aren't through changing yet.

31

Are there things that grownups do or say that bother you? Do you think you'll be different when you're a grownup? Answering the questions below may help you think about that. If you write the answers on a piece of paper, and stick them in a place where you save things, you'll get a chance to read them sometime later and see if any changes have taken place yet.

List three things you promise yourself you will not say or do to kids when you are a grownup.

1.

2.

3.

List three things that you think you should be able to do but can't, because you are a kid.

1.

2.

3.

Write about anything else you can think of about being a kid that you may want to remember later.

What about when your parents were kids? How did they feel about their families? Are they doing things differently now because of what their lives were like as kids? Or are they being grownups just like they remember their parents were? One way to find out is to ask your parents to fill out this form as they would have when they were your age. Ask them to think back and remember how it was for them then. Then compare your answers with theirs.

The Law at Home

Remember, because you are a minor, the law tries to protect you. At home too. Do you know how it does this? First of all, your parents have to support you, educate you, and control you. That's the law. They must do this until you are at least 16. That age isn't the same in all states, but 16 is the youngest possible age that their legal responsibility stops. The protection you get is that your parents can't decide that they no longer want to take care of you. And at the same time, you cannot decide that you no longer need them to take care of you.

What about this caring? What does it legally mean? Support first. That means you must be taken care of in terms of food, shelter, and health. That's an obligation of your parents. Education? Most states have laws that say you have to attend school between certain ages, like from 7 to 16. It's your parents' responsibility to make sure you go to school. They can legally insist that you have religious training also. Control you? Yup. They have total responsibility and authority to control you. There is only one thing the law says your parents cannot do to you and that is to endanger your safety or morals. What do you think "endanger your safety or morals" means? Ask your parents what they think it means.

32

Some more information. Along with their responsibilities, parents get some rights. Your parents have the right to services from you at home — chores and such. In a way, you are apprenticed to your parents, and they have the right to expect that you work. Legally, your father can control the kinds of friends you have. If you have a friend, and he doesn't think this friend is good for you in some way, he can ban the friend from your house. Your parents may control you with physical punishment, as long as it isn't "excessive, immoderate and unreasonable." If they do, they may be punished in criminal court. Parents have the right to any money you earn, even if you are living away from home. Did you know that? Do they? Do you want them to?

Your parents have another right. They can emancipate you. That means that you no longer can claim the right to their support. And they give up their rights to control you, require any service from you, or take any of your earnings. This is a tricky one. Remember your parents still have the legal responsibility to see that you are cared for. Both of you have to agree to you being emancipated. For example, they can emancipate you for a certain period of time, like during a summer when you have a job. They can emancipate you, and you can

still live at home. You could move out of the house and not necessarily be emancipated. You can't emancipate yourself. Only your parents can emancipate you. And you would still be legally bound to other restrictions of the law on minors that applied, such as compulsory education.

The legal bond between parents and their children is very strong and not to be easily destroyed. The law has tried to make rules so that parents and children can live together with as little conflict as possible.

What do you think about all this? Did you know about these legal rights and responsibilities? Do you think your parents know about them? Has the law affected you at home in any way that you can think of? Are there any parts of the law that you think ought to be changed? Would your parents agree with you?

Who Decides What?

It's clear from the law that your parents have a great deal of authority over your life. In your daily life, how does this power get used? What are the laws in your family that you have to abide by?

Enough questions. Here's a chance for you to compare how decisions get made in your family with how you think they ought to get made. Read the list of ten questions. Who makes the decision in each question, you or your parents? It may not be so easy to tell for each. For some of them, you may think that both you and your parents decide together. That's fine, but think a little more about this. If there were a disagreement between you and your parents on any one of them, who would have the final say? Who would really make the final decision? Record your answers on a sheet of paper like this:

How decisions get made	
My parents decide	I decide
1	
2	
3	
4	
5	
6	
7	
8	
9	
10	

1. Who decides what you eat?
2. Who decides the clothes you get?
3. Who decides who your friends are?
4. Who decides when you get your hair cut?
5. Who decides what time you go to bed?
6. Who decides how clean you keep your room?
7. Who decides how much TV you watch?
8. Who decides whether or not you can smoke?
9. Who decides what you read?
10. Who decides how you spend your money?

Now go through the list again. This time put how you think each decision *should be made* on another piece of paper like this:

How I think decisions should be made	
My parents should decide	I should decide
1	
2	
3	
4	
5	
6	
7	
8	
9	
10	

Now compare the two lists. If there are differences, then that may be where there is conflict in your family. What can be done about differences? The chapter on communication may give you some hints about ways to deal with things like this.

What Are the Laws of Your Family?

Do you know for sure what the rules are in your family? What you can and can't do? What's expected of you? What to do when there is a conflict?

Try this experiment. Make a list of all the family laws that you think of that everyone in your family would agree to. You may think that your family really doesn't have any laws. That things pretty well get taken care of somehow. Well then, push your thinking a little farther. Your family operates the way it does because there is some agreement on how things should run. A list of rules posted on the refrigerator is not always needed for people to know what they are. Remember that common law grew out of rules that people used over time.

David listed some of the rules in his house. One was that all the kids had to do their chores. Another was that they had to let their parents know where they were when they weren't home. And when someone was watching TV, you couldn't change the channel without their permission. With ten kids in the family, the TV rule seemed like a crucial one. There were other things everyone did also, like carry their own plates to the kitchen sink when they were finished eating. But the three rules David stated first seemed to be most important to his family right now.

Stephen felt that there was really only one family rule that he and his brother had to abide by. Here's how he said it. If you weren't where you told your parents you were going to be, then you had to let them know where you were instead. And his mom agreed with him that this was the one important family law.

When you've got your list made, check it out with the other people in your family and see if everyone agrees.

The history about the invention of kidhood, and the information about the laws that affect you at home may give you an overall understanding about why certain things in your family are the way they are. But they are only starting points.

What other factors make your family the family it is? And where do you as a kid fit into all these factors?

Don't answer the phone unless it's ringing. Psst! Hey!

Don't drink milk with a fork.

Don't feed the canary to the cat.

No sleeping on the ceiling.

Don't put the dog in the washing machine.

Don't wear other people's shoes on your ears. Huh?

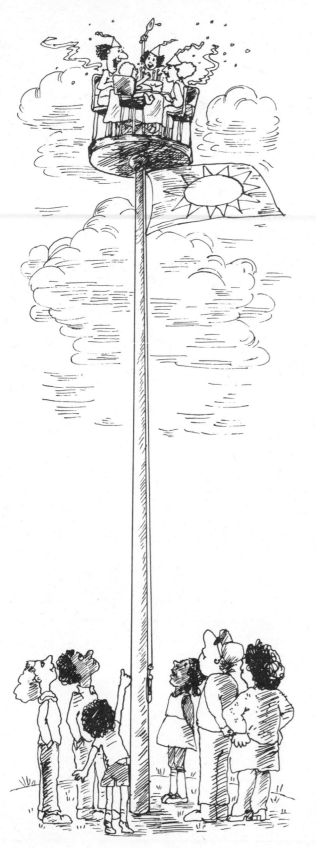

Your Family's Rituals

What does your family do together? Regularly? These are your family rituals. Rituals are activities that people do over and over again. Brushing your teeth every morning is a personal ritual. Eating supper together every night can be a family ritual. So can having Thanksgiving dinner with certain food every year, or celebrating birthdays in a special way, or observing religious occasions in your house.

Some rituals may be special with your family. Probably not many other families do them in the same way. A special way of doing something may have started in your family because someone thought it was a good idea. It caught on and became a ritual. Some rituals are ones which lots of other families do, too. They are rituals that weren't invented in your home — they're from society.

Here's an example. In Patrick's family, there have always been special rituals for celebrating birthdays for him and his brother Paul. There has always been a birthday cake. That part of the ritual wasn't invented in their home. The German people get the credit for first using a cake for a birthday celebration, candles and all. It was called a *geburtstagtorten*. But Patrick's cakes are always very special. His mom makes them in a very special way. Patrick is crazy about mon-

36

sters, and one year his mom made the cake so that it looked just like the Creature from the Black Lagoon. One year it was Ultraman. They tasted good too. Also on birthdays in this family, there is always a piñata. That's a Mexican ritual, one that their father carried over from when he was a kid. So Patrick's birthday rituals come from Germany, from Mexico, and from his own family, too.

Make a list of all the rituals you can think of that your family shares together. It may help to brainstorm this list with the rest of your family.

Once you've got a list, there are different ways you can explore it.

① Which of these are special to your family, ones that were begun in your family? Which are rituals that started from some influence outside your home, that other people share as well? Label the ones that began inside your family with an **F**. And label the ones that started in society in a larger sense with an **S**. Which are there more of?

② What rituals did your parents have in their families when they were kids? Ask them. How many of these did they carry on into your family today? Which ones don't you do in your family today? How come?

③ Which of the rituals are especially for kids? Which are especially for adults, but kids get to come along? Which are for both equally? What's the ritual balance in your family?

④ Check with your friends. Getting a picture of other families' rituals may help you get a clearer picture of your own.

There is no one way all families operate. There's no need for that. There are influences from society in general: holidays that families celebrate, customs that we observe. Some of these are special for our country. Some of them are religious. Yet there may be things that are your family's own special things to do. How much is your family life influenced by the larger world?

The Guest List

Who outside of your family comes to your house? How many visitors come in a week? Why do they come? To find out, make a guest sign-in sheet to keep track of who does come. A sign like this will help:

> I am doing an experiment about who comes to our house. Please sign your name to the list. Thanks!
>
> P.S. If you've already signed once, no need to sign again.

Put it on the door or some obvious place, so it's in clear view. Have a piece of paper near the sign and something to write with. This way you can keep track of who comes, even when you're in school or off somewhere else. Have people sign the list for an entire week, including the weekend.

How many of these people came mainly to see the grownups in the house? How many came mainly to see the kids? How many came to spend time with both grownups and kids? Sort them out and see. How many of the people were invited? How many just dropped in?

What does all this tell you about the traffic pattern of visitors to your house? Do you think this is typical for your friends' homes? Did you get the results you expected?

The Things in Your Family

Here are some "suppose situations." For each one, think about a possible solution that everyone in your family would agree to. Then check out your solutions with the rest of the family. It might be best to do this when the family is together. That way some discussion can help to iron out the differences.

SITUATION 1

Some wonderful, generous person thinks your family deserves a present. There's no limit on what the cost is, but the family must agree on one thing to buy for the house. What would your family pick?

SITUATION 2

Your family is moving to another country for a year or two. You'll be given a house with all the necessities in it — beds, furniture, stove, refrigerator. You can each take a suitcase for your personal needs. Your family can also decide to take three things from the house. What would your family take?

SITUATION 3

There's too much stuff in your house. Three big things have to go. Which three would your family decide to live without?

If there was a disagreement in any of these situations and no solution came from discussion, how would the problem get solved? Would one member of your family have the final say? Who would that be? How important are possessions to your family? How important are possessions to you?

What's Ahead

Your family isn't like a block of cement. It's more like clay. It can be strong and sturdy, but it can be changed at any time. Sometimes by a big crush, like a crisis that happens to one or more people in your family and affects everyone. Or by a little dent. Things in your family may seem just right at times, and perfectly miserable at other times. And as a kid you don't always have the power over your life that you would like. That's the way it is. But the clearer you are about understanding things that affect you from both inside the family and from the larger world, the closer you are to knowing what to do when you get the chance. And you will get the chance. You won't be a kid forever.

Chapter 5

The Scoop on School

Your education is your legal right, whether or not you want it. In most states you have to go to school between the ages of 7 and 16. That's a lot of years, and a lot of time each year. It's probably the most important way that grownups see to do their job of teaching you.

Who Runs the Schools?

There's a board of education for every school district. The people on the board of education are all grownups. That's no surprise. They meet regularly to oversee the schools. And they live in the school district. That's to keep what happens in school as close to home as possible.

Boards of education usually govern all the schools in a city, in a town, or in a group of smaller towns. But they do have to follow overall regulations set by the state. The state sets the age limits for compulsory education. The state sets general requirements for what you have to study. The state decides on standards for teachers.

But the board of education in your district makes the rules for your school. Teachers and principals enforce the school rules. Your teacher can also make extra rules that are reasonably necessary to do the job of educating you. And you have to follow all of them.

Are the Rules Clear?

Imagine that there's a new kid in your class. Your teacher gives you a job: teach this kid the rules — both the school rules and the special rules of your class. Could you do it?

Try it. Get a piece of paper and something to write with, and start your brain going. Write down any rules that you can think of. Big ones. Little ones. Even ones you're not sure count as rules. And when you're done, squeeze your brain a little more to see if there are any rules left in there.

Here's what to do with your list when you've got it made.

Could you teach a new kid all the special rules of your class?

1

Check with a friend or two in your class. See if they agree with your rules. Maybe they can add some. Put a mark next to the ones you can't really agree are rules. Check with someone else about them — another classmate, or your teacher.

2

Now read over the list again. This time mark the rules you think are school rules. The ones that all students follow no matter which class they're in. Then mark the other rules, the ones you think are made by your teacher for your class. Are you sure about them? Talk with your friends to see if they agree. Then check with your teacher.

3

Show your classroom rules to a friend who isn't in your class. Do your two classes have any of the same rules? Any different rules?

Five-year-olds usually start kindergarten. That's not generally required by the law, but most people feel it's a good way to ease kids into the first grade. It's a part-time preparation, a way to learn the rules and ropes of school. In some schools in Great Britain, all of the five-year-olds don't appear on the first day of school in September. They come on their birthdays. That way the teacher doesn't have to teach everyone the rules and ropes at the same time. The older kids are responsible for helping the newer ones feel comfortable. Do you think that's a good idea? Try to remember what the beginning of kindergarten was like for you and how you learned the rules.

Who Decides What You're Taught?

What you are taught in school is called the curriculum. The curriculum of your school is set by the board of education. There are usually some state requirements that have to be followed. There may even be required textbooks. And you've got to study what is set by the curriculum. That's part of the law.

What do you think you ought to learn in school? Stop a second. That's not an easy question. Not all grownups agree about the answer, not all teachers do, either. You go to school for at least twelve years. When you finish high school, what do you think you ought to know?

Is it necessary for you to go to school to learn these things you need to know? How come you can't stay home and learn instead? Well, school serves more than just you. It serves your parents too. Your parents are responsible for your education. That's part of their responsibilities according to the law. And if you didn't go to school, they'd have that job to do along with everything else in

their lives. How do you think they would feel about that? How do you think your parents would feel about having you around all day? Every day.

Think about what your parents would teach you. Put your thoughts into three lists like this:

List 1. Things my parents would teach me that are the same things I learn about in school.

List 2. Things my parents would teach me that I don't learn about in school.

List 3. Things my parents would not teach me that I learn about in school now.

When you've got your lists made, here are some ways to explore your lists.

1. Check your lists with your parents. That will give you some information about what they value about your schooling.

2. Sort your lists. Put a star ★ next to your favorite things to learn about. Put a circle ⊙ next to the ones you really don't like, the ones you wish no one had ever invented. Put an ✗ next to those you think you could live your life without and not miss a thing, even when you're an adult. Now look over the way you sorted your lists. This will give you a look at what you value about your schooling.

43

The law says that teachers and principals are "in loco parentis" when you are in school. That means that they can act like your parents when you're in their charge. They can do whatever is reasonably necessary to do their job of educating you. And legally they can use any punishment as long as it's reasonable. Until recently, physical punishment was legally OK for schools. Now some states have passed laws that forbid it. Some school districts which are not in those states have also made that rule. How do you feel about that? Do you think all physical punishment should be forbidden in schools? How are the rules in your school enforced?

When someone in your class breaks a rule, what does the teacher do? What is the worst punishment the teacher gives? Do you think these punishments are reasonably necessary in order for your teacher to get on with the job of helping kids learn?

What's the worst punishment your teacher gives?

Here's a list of things you might do in class. Suppose each one was against some rule. You get to decide how serious you think each one is. Here's the code to use:

A means — very serious

B means — pretty serious

C means — kind of serious

D means — no big deal

Number from 1 to 7 on a piece of paper, and as you read the list, give each one an A, B, C, or D.

1. Throw a paper wad.

2. Come in late.

3. Not pay attention.

4. Not do an assignment.

5. Copy someone else's assignment, because you didn't have time to do it.

6. Copy someone else's assignment because you didn't want to do it.

7. Make fun of someone who answered a question wrong.

Look at how you sorted them. Which ones stop your learning if you do them? Which ones stop someone else's learning? Did this matter when you graded them?

If a kid does something totally unacceptable in school, what's the worst punishment that kid could get? Suppose there were no punishments of any kind allowed in school. How would that affect your education?

How Do the Laws Protect You?

Laws about minors have mostly been set up to protect you. How does this apply to school? Are you given any protection when you are a student, or do you just turn over your body and mind when you arrive at school — just to get the job done. This is one area of the law that's been getting a lot of attention in recent years.

Here are some examples. The law says that teachers and principals can do whatever is reasonably necessary in order to do their job of educating you. There was a time when girls were not allowed to wear pants to school. They had to wear skirts or dresses. This was probably the way it was when your parents were in school. You can check this out with them. There was a time when long hair on boys became a big issue in schools.

There were students who disagreed with these rules. And sometimes their parents did too. Some of these became legal arguments that wound up in court to be decided. And in these cases, courts have said that the rules were unreasonable. That the only time a rule is reasonable is if it's necessary for *educating* the students. It's hard to imagine how long hair on boys could stop their learning. It never seems to clog up girls' ears or brains. And there's no reason why girls wearing pants can't learn as well as girls wearing skirts. Besides, it's a lot more practical in cold weather and much more comfortable on the playground.

The Story of the Tinker Family

Sometimes a decision about students' rights has been so important that the Supreme Court decides to listen to the disagreement and make a decision. The Supreme Court is the highest court in the United States. It only considers matters which are very, very important. This decision was made in 1969.

The problem started in 1965. The Tinkers were a family that lived in Iowa. They were very much against the war in Vietnam at that time. They felt so strongly about this, they decided to publicly show their feelings. They decided to wear black armbands during the Christmas season as a symbol of how they felt.

The Des Moines school district, where the Tinker kids went to school, didn't want kids wearing black armbands. They passed a rule against it. But the kids wore them anyway. And they were suspended. They were not allowed to go back to school until they stopped protesting.

The family was angry about this. They felt that the school decision violated their freedom of speech. The school felt that the rule was necessary to avoid a disturbance of discipline. The argument went to a federal court. In 1966 that court upheld the school's position.

Finally the case got to the Supreme Court. There the decision was reversed. It was a close five-to-four vote, but the Tinkers won. The court did not feel that wearing black armbands meant disruption of discipline. The court said that students, just like adults, have the constitutional right to freedom of expression of their beliefs.

This was an important decision. It has had an effect on other such disagreements. A Supreme Court decision is a final decision. Schools need to consider that decision when they look at their rules. That decision makes an important statement about your constitutional rights and the rules of your school.

Congress Gets in the Act

The federal government doesn't make many laws about schools. It's the state governments that have the big responsibility there. But here's a situation that Congress decided was important enough to pass an act. It had to do with your school records and was signed into law on New Year's Eve in 1974.

Do you know what your school records are? They follow you through your school life, and often after that. Each year, your teacher writes a report on how you did. Test scores are included, grades, comments about your behavior, whatever the teacher or principal or counselor or nurse or other school person feels is important. For many years, neither you nor your parents could see your records. This law changed that.

Now, up until you are 18, your parents can see any of your records. After you are 18, only you can see them. No one outside your school authorities has automatic rights to take even one peek, unless they have written permission from you. Before you are 18, your parents give the written permission.

Here's a possible reason for this. Suppose when you were in the fifth grade you managed to get into a bunch of trouble in school. Maybe your parents had just gotten a divorce, and you were too upset to do anything you were supposed to. Maybe your best friend was in your class, and the two of you goofed off so much you never did much work and were really problems. Maybe you had just moved and you were really unhappy about that and acted as awful as you felt. Your teacher was displeased enough so that when it came time for completing your yearly record, all this bad behavior was put in. Then you go on to the sixth grade and the new teacher reads your record. Maybe by then you've changed a lot. That could be a rotten way to start a new year. Suppose that years later you are applying to a college and even though you were in fifth grade a long time ago, you're afraid your record might affect this application.

Under the new law, you or your parents could see what was in the record. And you could petition to have any material removed from your record that is damaging or not proved. The school must have some way to hear your side. And if they decide against you, they must at least enter in your record that you disagreed and that you challenged it.

These decisions may not seem to have much effect on your school life so far. That's super. But remember that some of the rights you have in school came about because of long brave fights by people who felt very strongly about some issue. Laws are meant to serve people's lives. They're not supposed to make lives unreasonably difficult. And when a law no longer makes sense, someone has to get a change started.

There's more to your school life than the law, like what goes on inside your class and inside your head every day. And even though the rules in your school are made and enforced by the grownups in charge, you are the one really responsible for what goes on inside your head. Here's one way to explore that.

How Do You Learn Best?

Suppose you are going to learn something new. You're going to make something that you've never made before — something out of wood. Maybe a box for all those little things you like to save that are scattered around your room at home. Maybe a container for all your felt-tip markers. Maybe a stand to prop up books when you're reading. Think of something you might like to make.

47

How would you get started? Which of these ways would be best?

Way 1: Get some wood, a saw, a hammer, and some nails and go to work.

Way 2: Think of someone who knows about building things out of wood. Get them to help.

Way 3: Go to the library and check out a book, like *Woodworking for Absolutely Anyone,* written especially for kids.

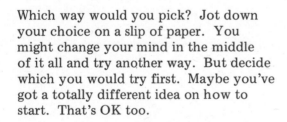

Which way would you pick? Jot down your choice on a slip of paper. You might change your mind in the middle of it all and try another way. But decide which you would try first. Maybe you've got a totally different idea on how to start. That's OK too.

Suppose you were going to learn a different thing, like your seven-times table. Or some other multiplication facts you don't know well enough. Read the ways below. Which way would you start? Write your choice under your other one.

Way 1: Just start studying them, looking at the list over and over, saying them to yourself. Learn them by yourself.

$7 \times 7 = 49$, $7 \times 8 = 56$

Way 2: Get someone to help you. A friend to quiz you or a parent to go over them with you.

"7×4 = ?" "28" "7×5 = ?" "35" "7×6"

Way 3: Get something else to help you, maybe a stack of flash cards, maybe a record of multiplication facts, or a tape recording you could listen to.

$4 \times 3 = 12$

Now repeat $4 \times 4 =$ $4 \times 5 =$ 4×6

Still another possibility to learn. Suppose you got a new bicycle and it came in a shipping carton and had to be assembled. Again, write down which way you would start.

Way 1: Take all the pieces out, look them over and start with what seems sensible.

Way 2: Ask someone you think knows how to do it to help you — a friend, an older brother or sister, a parent.

Way 3: Read the instructions first. Then follow them step-by-step.

One more possible thing to learn. Something physical that you've seen done, but have never learned yourself. Something new in gymnastics, like a cartwheel or front flip, or a yoga exercise. Mark down your choice.

Way 1: Try doing it yourself.

Way 2: Ask someone to teach you — maybe a friend who knows how to do it and knows how to be patient too.

Way 3: Get a book that explains the exercise with photographs and try to learn it that way.

In each case you were imagining learning a different kind of thing, so different skills were needed. The ways for learning were also different for each thing. But notice this. Way 1 for each was to do it all by yourself, relying on just you. Way 2 was to get help from another person. Way 3 was to get help from some other source, but not another person.

Look at your choices. Did you choose the same way for each situation? If you did, that tells you something about your own style of learning something new, no matter what it is. Did you pick different ways for the different experiments?

You may have different ways of learning different kinds of things. The first experiment was making something new using your hands. The second was getting your mind to soak up some facts you needed. The third was doing something mechanical, a kind of step-by-step operation. The fourth was learning to do something physical, where your body also learns something new, not just your head.

There is no one best way to get started doing any of these. But it's not enough for you just to know how you'd choose to learn in these examples. What's more important is that you can learn about yourself as a learner, about the way you learn things best.

This could be a help in school. Suppose you think you learn best when you work with one other person. Maybe that's not the way your teacher has you learn certain things in class. Your class might be organized so kids work alone or in larger groups of six kids together. You might make a request like this. "I've been thinking about how I learn best. I think it's when I learn with one other person. Could I do this next time we learn something new — like our spelling words?"

Your teacher may agree. Hurray for you. Your teacher may ask how come you think you learn best that way. How would you explain that? Your teacher may say no, that it's not possible. That you'll have to do it the way the rest of the class does. And that's that.

Suppose you were the teacher, and a kid came to you with this request. Think about how you might handle it.

Have you ever thought about what it must be like to be a teacher? You've got a whole class of kids. They all like and dislike different things. Different kids learn best in different ways. There's lots to do.

Teachers have been specially trained in college to do their jobs. But they don't always learn everything they need in their college training. Is that a great surprise to you? Do you think you'll learn all you need to know in school?

Here's a chance to try one part of what it's like to be a teacher. You need to pretend that you are a teacher. If that seems totally impossible, try imagining you are going to do it just for the next few paragraphs.

50

The Colossal
I-Don't-Have-a-Pencil
Problem

There is a problem that teachers all have to face sometime. And they have to decide what to do about it, so they don't go totally bats in the classroom. The problem: what to do when a kid says, "I don't have a pencil."

Does this happen in your class? If not, maybe your teacher has a good solution. What do you do if you don't have a pencil?

Now maybe this doesn't seem like a really important part of a teacher's job. Your teacher is supposed to be helping you learn, not worrying about pencils. How does worrying about pencils help you learn? Well, you answer that one.

What would you do about kids who don't have pencils, and they tell you just when you're about to give the first word of the spelling test? Think of as many solutions to the problem as you can. Then decide which you think would least interrupt the kids' learning. Maybe you could share your thinking with your teacher. You might be doing a big service.

What other problems, like this one, do teachers face that get in the way of teaching kids? Try making a list called Everyday Problems That Can Drive the Teacher Nutty. See how you would solve them. It might help you decide if you'll ever become a teacher.

The Total Picture

Remember, the control over your school life is not in your hands. Your parents have the responsibility of educating you, and they've turned a big part of that job over to the schools.

There may be parts of school that you think are really OK. There may be things about school that you like a lot, that are important to your life. There may be other things about school that you're not crazy about, but you kind of understand why they are necessary. But maybe you've been going to school and never thinking about why certain things are done for you and to you.

And then there are times when you may bump up against situations in school that make no sense to you. You may be able to find ways to influence those decisions. Even change them. But, in the end, you're the student and the rules rule you. The school expects certain things of you and has the right to do so. *Later* is coming. And when *later* gets here, you'll have a lot more control about what you learn. You'll get to be the one to decide what you expect from you.

Chapter 6

Dollars and Sense

Money seems to be important to everyone. People talk about it a lot. Argue about it. Spend it. Save it. Gamble with it. Write books about it. Some people let it slip through their fingers. Others try to make it stretch. Some say that money is the root of all evil. Do you know any of those people?

Try a poll. Ask your parents why money is so important. Ask other grownups.

What about you? When did money first seem important to you? How old were you then? Check with your friends to see if they agree. Who controls the money in your life?

Checking Out Your Financial Situation

Here's a questionnaire about money. Over 100 kids who live in the San Francisco Bay Area filled out this questionnaire. They were between the ages of 9 and 13. Jot down how you would answer these questions on a piece of paper. Then you can compare your financial situation with the kids in California who also filled out the questionnaire.

1. Where do you get money?

	Yes or No	How Often	How Much
Allowance			
Earnings			
Gifts			
Special request to your parents			

2. Are there things your parents say you have to spend your money on? If so, what for?

3. Think about the last time you bought something with your money that was not something to eat. How much did you spend? What did you buy?

4. If you ask your parents for money for something special, what do you usually need it for?

5. Do you have a piggy bank or some bank at home you keep money in? If you do, about how much is in it now?

6. Do you have money in a bank account? If so, how much is in it? Do you have control over it?

7. Who are you usually with when you buy the following:

	Parent	Friend	Brother or Sister	Alone
Shoes				
Something over $10				
Something $4-$6				
Something $.50-$1.50				
Snacks				

8. Are you saving money now? For something special to buy? How much does it cost?

9. Suppose someone gave you $10 right now. What would you do with it?

Here are the results from the kids in the San Francisco area.

1. All kids got money from somewhere. *Allowance:* 83% Yes, an average of $1.00 a week. *Earnings:* 66% Yes, an average of $1.00 a week. *Gifts:* 84% Yes, an average of three times a year, $10 was the average amount. *Special Request:* 77% Yes, a couple of times a month, $2-$3 a month total.

2. Most kids (78%) did not have to spend their money on anything special.

3. The things kids spent their money on most often that were not food were presents, clothes, books, hobbies, bicycle parts, movies, pet supplies, records, field trips.

4. When kids asked their parents for money for something special, it was for things like presents, sports equipment, hobby supplies, models, books, games, records, movies, sports events, field trips. They also spent their own money on these things and seemed to ask when they had run out.

5. 83% of the kids had piggy banks at home. Their savings went from 10 cents to $60, with a $10 average.

6. About two-thirds of the kids had bank accounts. There was a big difference in amounts, depending on whether only the kids put money in it or if their parents did too. Of the kids who had bank accounts, 68% answered that they did not have control over the money in it.

7. When buying shoes, 94% of the kids went with their parents. And almost 70% went with their parents for purchases of $10 or more. But when buying stuff that cost $1.50 or less, or for snacks, kids were mostly alone or with friends.

8. Three-fourths of the kids were saving money. When asked if they were saving for something special, over half answered yes. The kids that were saving for something special wanted things like records, clothes, a TV, ten-speed bicycle, dirt bike, tape recorder, camera, skateboard.

9. About two-thirds of the kids said they would save it, either for something special or just to save. Other kids thought they would spend it on toys, books, games, records, clothes, or hobby supplies. A few answered that they'd save half and spend the rest.

What does all this say? Kids do have money to spend and they get to spend a lot of it on their own without accounting to their parents.

How did your financial survey compare with the results given here? How do you think your money life compares with your friends? How important is your money to you? Do you think you have enough money for your needs?

What the Law Says About Your Money

What about your legal rights and money? How does the law try to protect you? Kids can legally own property. That also means you can own money that is given to you. It's true that your parents have the right to any money you earn. But if they decide not to take that money, then it is your property, just like a gift. So far so good. Even though it is your money, your parents do control you, legally, and may make some demands on what you do or don't do with your money. Although the law says you can have money of your own, it's the rules of your family which have more effect on your financial life.

What about savings accounts? There is no legal reason why you can't have an account that is all yours, without having either of your parent's name on it. But the bank doesn't have to let you have an account in your own name. They may insist that your parents get in on the act. They may insist on this even if your parents agree that you can be responsible for your own savings. What can you do then? Not much, at least at that bank. If it is important to you to have an account that is independently yours, try another bank.

Do you know about checking accounts? That's when you put your money in the bank, but not to save it and have it earn money for you by collecting interest. This is an account for money that you intend to use frequently. When you write a check to pay for something, the person who receives it from you can get the actual money from a bank. That way, you don't have to carry money around. And it's safer than having a huge wad of money crumpled up in your pocket. People who pay bills regularly, usually have checking accounts. They don't use checks often for small purposes. You have to pay the bank for this service, often 10 cents or so for the blank check itself. So it doesn't make sense to use it for a small amount. It just costs you extra and makes extra work for everyone. But if you have regular bills to pay, it's handy. You can legally have a checking account of your own. This is pretty unusual for kids, and the bank has the right to say no. So if you venture into a bank to ask, prepare yourself for a nervous chuckle from the new accounts person — or even a smirk. But maybe it's worth a try, if it's important and useful to you.

If you were a bank manager, how do you think you would feel about a kid having a savings account or a checking account? If you can think of some reasons why it's a fine idea, you might be better at explaining yourself, if you decide to open one.

You Are Big Business

Kids between the ages of 8 and 12 spend more than two billion dollars each year. That makes you an important consumer. Grownups have noticed that. The President's Committee on Consumer Interests has, for example. The committee made a statement that being a skilled consumer is important for everyday living and that kids need to be well prepared. Advertisers have noticed you. They spend an enormous amount of money each year convincing kids to buy. Most of that money is spent on TV. School people have paid attention to you. Books, posters, filmstrips, and movies have been developed for teachers to use with their classes on consumer education. (Have you had any consumer education in school?) Laws have been made to protect you in matters of spending money. And your parents too. They have to live with you, so they can't help but notice that you are an important consumer. Especially when you announce the things you just *have to* have.

Kids have become a powerful group of consumers. And the grownups in the world feel that they've got something to tell you about that. But they don't always agree with each other. Advertisers give you very special information about what they think you ought to do with your money. Your parents may give you just the opposite information.

The information or advice you get about how to spend your money is your *consumer information*. What kind of consumer are you? Where do you get information about what you want to buy? How can you learn to be a wise spender?

Here's an exercise to size up your consumer habits. For each question, you rank the choices. That means to decide which you think is the best choice, the next best, and down to the one you like the least. There are no right or wrong answers. Your answers will give you clues to your consumer practices. It may help if you think of some purchase you've made recently when you answer the questions. Not a snack, but something you bought to use.

1

Which influences you most to buy something?
• A friend has one and likes it.
• You saw it advertised on TV or somewhere else.
• You saw one somewhere and it looked good.

2

Sometimes you get something new and it breaks really quickly. Why do you think this generally happened?
• It wasn't made very well.
• You were too rough with it.
• You used it incorrectly.

3

If you bought something that broke too easily, what would you do?
• Try to fix it.
• Throw it away.
• Take it back to the store.

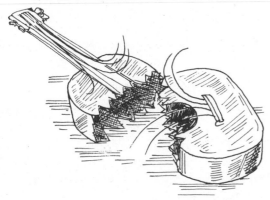

4

Suppose you decided to buy something and there were different models to choose from. How would you decide?
• Ask a salesperson in the store.
• Read the box it came in.
• Ask a friend who has one.
• Ask one of your parents.
• Buy the one you saw on TV.

5

What do you think is true about most advertisements?
• Advertisements are a helpful way to learn about stuff you might want.
• Advertisements don't tell you the truth about products.
• Advertisements do their job of getting you to spend your money.

Is there any way to be really sure when you are making a purchase? Probably not. Even when you ask people who are interested in helping you to make a wise choice, you may get different answers. Their feelings may help you, but facts are important.

To Buy or Not to Buy

How do advertisers get you to think about their products? How do they try to convince you that their products are better than the rest?

They've got their methods. Carefully thought out. Tested on thousands. Planned to get you to spend your money where they want you to. They want you to remember their products, and here are some of their techniques.

Technique 1. Catchy Slogans. It may be in a tune or in a rhyme, or it may be just clever and easy to remember. It's designed to be a handy reminder of the product. It makes the advertisers' hearts warm to hear people humming their jingles.

Technique 2. It's a Deal. The advertisement tries to show you what a good bargain the product is, how it will save you money. The key words: bargain, save, sale.

Technique 3. Everyone Wants One. This method can almost make you feel weird or left out if you don't have one. The advertiser tries to convince you that because so many other people have bought it, you should too.

Technique 4. You'll Be Special. This method attracts you by having a famous person talk about the product. The hint is, if you like this person, then buy the product.

Technique 5. Your Life Will Be Better. A skit may show people doing something exciting. The advertisers want you to think that your life will be more exciting, if you get one. You'll have more fun, more adventure, romance.

Technique 6. The Friendly Approach. This method shows regular looking people on the street, in their homes, or in stores. They don't look much like actors or actresses. It aims at making the message believable.

Technique 7. The Fancy Language Method. This one uses scientific-type words you probably don't even know. The technical terms are supposed to give you the impression that scientific methods were used in making this product.

Technique 8. Your Life Will Be Easier. This product works more easily, faster, and will probably last longer than others. How have you lived this long without it? That's what the advertiser would like you to think.

There are advertisements in magazines, newspapers, on billboards, buses, trains, store windows, radio, and TV. Try to think of some advertisements that you have seen somewhere. What made you remember those in particular?

Next time you're watching TV, see if you can find advertisements that fit these techniques. Keep the list handy and after you watch a commercial, check to see if one of these methods was used. If not, try to figure out what technique was used.

Which of the techniques are especially used in commercials for kids? Try the experiment both in the evening and during TV time that is mainly for kids. See if there are differences in the ways advertisers try to appeal to kids.

Talk with your parents about these techniques. Find out which they think are most effective. Watch their reactions to commercials to see which ones they seem to respond to. Then the next time you'd like them to buy something for you, maybe you can sell them the idea with the right technique. You might get some benefit from all the research advertisers have done on how to get people to spend their money.

In an average day, the average person is exposed to 1,600 advertisements. The advertisements are not free information, either. You are the one who pays for them. When you buy something, 20 to 40% of the price of the item goes for the advertising. You are paying that.

61

The Federal Trade Commission reviews about half a million TV and radio advertising scripts and about a quarter of a million pages of ads that appear in print each year. About 40,000 of them are checked further. That's because advertisers cannot present false information in their ads. But that doesn't mean they necessarily have to give you *all* the information. Imagine a soft drink advertisement telling you that not only does their bubbly drink taste terrific, it also rots your teeth.

Advertisers sometimes prefer half-truths to whole truths. What can you do as a consumer? Keep your wits about you. Compare prices. Read information on labels and packages carefully. Check the *Consumer Reports* magazines in your library to find out what advertisers don't tell you about their products.

Putting Your Mouth Where Your Money Is

What about when you buy something you saw advertised, you try it, and you feel like you've really been gypped? It didn't work the way it was supposed to. It had parts missing; even if it's just the battery it needs to run on. Or you think it didn't live up to the advertiser's claims.

This happens sometimes when you send away for something in the mail, like models of an entire army, complete with tanks and trucks and jeeps. And the whole collection arrives in a box barely big enough to stuff a pair of socks into. Go read that advertisement again. What technique did they use that got you so interested, you forgot to read the part about how big the pieces were? And now you've got an army that couldn't defend the top of your dresser. Not much you can do.

But what about if the advertisement claimed something about the product that just isn't true? You could write to the company. That's a hassle. There are agencies you could write to. One is the Bureau of Consumer Protection, Federal Trade Commission, Washington, D. C. 20580. They get several thousand complaint letters a year, and they do have an effect on advertisements. They won't get your money back for you, though. Or you can check in the white pages of your telephone book under Consumer Complaints. There may be several numbers listed for different purposes. It's a tough go. And all because there was some nifty item you thought you'd enjoy owning.

Suppose you bought it in a store. Take it back and complain. Some hints if you do that. Don't complain to the wrong person. It won't help telling the high school kid working at the cash register. If you think you ought to tell your story for practice, try it out on a more receptive listener. Don't lose your temper. Explain how you feel and why. Ask for a refund. If this doesn't do any good, for sure find some other place to spend your money next time.

Where's the Law Now?

This seems the time for a bit of legal protection. True. You've got some coming. The law is very definite about how you are protected in business transactions, and whenever you buy something, you are making a business transaction. The law is set up to protect you from more experienced business people who may take advantage of you. It also protects you from your own lousy judgment by allowing you to change your mind in a business deal. It's a bit tricky to understand.

As a minor, you cannot make a contract and legally be held to it. A contract is an agreement between people. When you agree to buy something, you are making a contract. But you can change your mind. Even if you've already paid for it. This discourages grownups from dealing with you. It doesn't mean you can't go into a store and make a sizable purchase, like a tape recorder or a ten-speed bike. Lots of grownups are willing to do business with you and will cheerfully take your money. But they are taking a risk. How do they know you won't smash your new bike into a tree and then return it because it is unsatisfactory? According to the law, they have to give you your money back. They may choose to call your parents before coughing up a refund. You'd have to deal with that one. But the law is set up to protect you.

Here's another example. Your friend has a pocket calculator, but got a new, fancier one for her birthday. So you agree to buy the old one for $5. You give her the money, but when you get home, you realize that it's the kind that only works when it's plugged in, not with batteries. You decide to change your mind and get your money back. Your friend has to give it back. If she doesn't, you have grounds for taking legal action. This can be a complicated matter necessitating a lawyer. And being a minor, you'd need to have your parents get involved with that process.

But your friend is a minor also. Suppose the situation were different. You like the calculator you bought. But the next day she decides she'd rather give the old calculator to her brother, so he'll stop pestering her to use her new one. She could insist that you bring it back and give you your money back.

If you had bought the calculator from your friend's older brother, who was no longer a minor, he wouldn't have the same right to demand that you return the calculator. The law is designed to protect you. When you are no longer a minor, you are supposed to know enough to protect yourself.

There's one catch. (Watch out for legal catches.) There is one situation where even as a minor you could be held to your part of the deal in a contract. That's when you are buying something that is considered a "necessary." Then you are obligated just like any grownup. Whoever sold it to you is protected against you changing your mind.

But it turns out I don't like raisins.

RAISIN BREAD

Try making a list of things you think are "necessaries." The law doesn't make a clean list. Things you use for food, shelter, or clothing are most likely necessaries. But not always. A warm jacket for winter is necessary, but not if you already have one, for example.

How do you feel about this protection that the law gives you? People usually make contracts with the intention of keeping their agreements. And here the law says that you are legally not responsible. It's protection, sure. But it can also limit you. Taking out a loan would be very hard for you to do. Even if you were able to prove you could repay it, you couldn't legally be held to your promise. The price for protection is a limit on your business freedom. And you, as a kid, have a legal reputation for being allowed not to keep up your end of a bargain.

Back to the storekeeper. If you get in a hassle where you are not being treated fairly and want to change your mind and return a purchase, then you might try informing the store owner about the law. The owner might give you your money back just to avoid trouble.

A Last Thought

Money is going to be an important influence in your life forever. Now's the time to start doing some thinking about what part you want it to play in your life. You may not be in total control of your actual financial situation, but you are in control of your mind. Give it some careful thought.

A consumer quickie. Which would you rather buy: Two candies for a nickel or three for a dime?

Never underestimate the power of some careful reasoning.

Chapter 7

Kids at Work

Do you ever find your allowance eaten up by your regular weekly spending? Maybe you have been eating up your allowance and still feel hungry. When you made a request for an increase, the source of your allowance just stared at you and gave you one of those money-doesn't-grow-on-trees lectures.

Have you ever considered getting a job? Well, then you need some information. Remember, minors are different from grownups. And minors who have worked have gotten a lot of special attention that may affect you.

Laying Out the Law

Here's what the law has to say about you as a working person. You are carefully protected by the law. Very carefully protected. You are protected from what the law calls "oppressive child labor." That means work that is in any way cruel, that can in any way cause you physical

or mental damage. Grownups argued for a long time about whether or not you were going to get this protection. And now, not only do all states have certain regulations, the federal government has some very serious things to say too.

The federal government first. There is a law called the Fair Labor Standards Act. It was passed by the federal government in 1938. This law makes "oppressive child labor" very specific. No one under the age of 18 can work at any job that is possibly harmful. There's a long list of those jobs. Here are some: any kind of mining, manufacturing and storing of explosives, operating dangerous machines

65

(including power-driven saws, bakery machines, power-driven hoisting machines), roofing, wrecking and demolition, slaughtering and meat-packing, driving a motor vehicle, street-selling, and dangerous exhibitions such as certain circus acts. There are more conditions to the most recent federal regulations. Sixteen is the youngest you can be to have a full-time job. Fourteen and fifteen year olds can work outside of school hours, though there are limits on the number of hours and a ban on nighttime hours. The job has to be a safe one. You can't work in a factory no matter what. Kids of any age can work in agriculture outside of school hours. If the agricultural work is dangerous, you have to be at least sixteen and you have to be paid the minimum wage that any worker can be paid, grownups included.

Does all this sound pretty reasonable to you? There were grownups who had to fight and argue for years to get these regulations passed. There were other grownups who felt that whether or not a kid worked was no business of the federal government. It was up to the parents and that the federal government had no business butting its nose into family decisions.

This was one of those snags where grownups saw things very differently and took a long time to finally reach an agreement. And where were kids during that time? Working.

Kids Working Has a Long History

There was a time when all kids worked. That was the way it was in colonial times. It was expected. Maybe your family lived on a farm. When you were old enough to help, you were given some jobs to do. The older you got, the more you got to do. Your parents taught you. They also watched out for you. They saw to it that you didn't do stuff that was dangerous.

Families had to do more than just farm to support themselves. Besides, there was no farming to do during the cold winter months in the North. So people made things. Some made furniture; some made sailing ships. Men did these things, and their sons came along and learned. Their help was useful to their fathers. Some families made cloth. The women and the children did the spinning; the men did the weaving.

It wasn't an easy life then. Families still grew their own food on their land. They worked long hours and hard hours.

And the kids knew that they were doing important work — work that helped to support the whole family.

There was another way kids worked. They were apprenticed to another household. That way they could learn a skill that their parents didn't have. They'd live in this other house. Sometimes they would be apprenticed as young as six or seven.

Inventions Change the World

In the middle of the 1700s, all this changed. Some important inventions were made. Machines were invented in England that could do the spinning and weaving of cloth as well as people could. The cotton gin was invented and could do the work of 50 people in separating cotton fibers from the seed coverings. Steam engines were made that could drive all the machinery.

This caused colossal changes. Factories were built in the North. So families who had been making cloth at home now went to work in the factories. More cotton began to be grown in the South. The slave trade from Africa was increased to provide labor for the southern plantations. Fuel was needed for the steam engines, so coal mines became very busy.

And what were the kids doing during these changes? Working.

This was a lot different than the work they had been doing at home or as apprentices.

Billy was one of the kids who had helped his family make cloth at home. Now he worked in a textile factory. The year was 1810. Billy's workday began at seven. He really rushed to get there too, because if he was even one minute late, he'd be docked an hour's pay. His job was to watch the huge spools, called bobbins, which held thread. Bobbins were kept on a rack up above the looms. If the thread broke, Billy had to tie it. If the spools ran out, he had to put up new ones. And to do this, he had to climb up on the machines. They were pretty rickety. If Billy wasn't careful, he could slip and fall to the ground or into the machines. That happened often. So he went barefoot. It was easier not to slip that way. He had a half-hour at noon to eat lunch. Billy's parents worked there too, and his mother packed some lunch for the family. At the end of the day he went home. That was at seven. He was tired, achy and his ears were full of the clanging of the machines. Sometimes Billy was too exhausted to eat. He did this six days a week.

Sometimes his boss got real mad and complained about the kids working in the factory. He said kids seemed to want to play more than work. Sometimes they even fell asleep on the job. There was a whipping room in some mills, and they'd take kids there if they weren't working fast enough.

The Grownups Begin to Argue

Some grownups who saw what was happening began to get very upset. This is no way for children to grow up, they thought. They should be in school. Long, hard work like this isn't healthy for growing kids. Those grownups knew that kids hardly got paid anything, but because they worked so cheaply, they got hired instead of men. So the kids sometimes were the main support of the family. It all seemed like a crazy bad dream.

Nonsense, others said. The kids are lucky to have work. It keeps them out of trouble. They'll learn the value of money. They'll learn what hard work really is. Besides, they're helping to build our country. What's bad about that?

Some laws did get passed in some states. By 1853 seven states had laws. Mostly they said that kids under the ages of 12 or 14 couldn't work more than ten hours a day. These laws didn't do much good. No one ever thought to appoint inspectors to make sure the laws were being followed. The first inspectors ever appointed were in 1867; that was 14 years after the laws were made.

After the Civil War, there was another industrial spurt. In 1870, 13% of all ten- to fifteen-year-olds were employed full-time outside the home.

The Kids Still Work

If you were a kid at that time, you could have been working in a coal mine. John was a coal breaker. That's what boys under 12 did. It was dirty work. The job was to sit on a low wooden plank in front of chutes where sharp-edged lumps of coal were dumped. Railroad cars were waiting for the coal. John had to get out the pieces of slate that were mixed in. It was horrible work. He was hunched over the chutes. Coal dust made his eyes burn. His fingers got cut and bruised easily from the sharp coal. Wearing gloves made him work too slowly. There was a good chance that John would grow up with a crooked backbone.

By 1900, 18% of all ten- to fifteen-year-old children were employed. That was about 1,700,000 kids. Of them 60% did agricultural work. And kids younger than ten worked too.

Ruby was seven in 1914. She picked cotton. From sunup to sundown. She was able to pick 35 pounds of cotton a day. Can you imagine how much feathery cotton it takes to make 35 pounds? On another farm, Mellie worked the same way. She picked about 30 pounds a day. She was five years old. Days were not much fun for these girls.

Jane's family worked doing piecework and she had to help. This was the kind of work people did in their own homes. They worked for clothing manufacturers. The clothing would get cut in the factory and people would pick it up and take it home to do one particular piece of the sewing. Maybe sewing on buttons. Maybe putting in linings. Jane's parents were paid by how much they got done. The employer would threaten not to give them any more work to do, if they didn't work fast enough. And her parents needed the work, so they worked long hours. Jane's job was to pull out all the basting threads. "Keep working," her father would snap when she fell asleep on her pile. "If we don't finish this soon, we won't get any more." It wasn't that Jane's father didn't love her. He just didn't know what else he could do to feed her and the rest of the family.

Why do you think parents allowed their children to work like this? For two reasons. The parents worked under the same conditions. And the money was badly needed.

The Fight Goes On

People continued to work to end these conditions. It was a long, hard, slow fight. Some people worked to get states to pass child labor laws. Some worked to get compulsory education laws passed. Some worked to get a federal law passed to protect all children in the country.

The Federal Government Takes Action

In 1916 a federal law was finally passed. It said that kids had to be at least 16 to work in the mines. That kids had to be at least 14 to do other kinds of work. That kids under 16 could work no more than eight hours a day, not at all at night, and had to have at least one day a week off.

But in 1918, the Supreme Court of the United States said that Congress had no power to pass a law like that. Congress tried again. A similar law was passed in 1919. The court said no to that one as well.

It seemed that the only way to get some federal legislation was to change the constitution. So Congress tried that in 1924. To change the constitution, three-fourths of the states have to agree to the change.

Incredible agruments went on. The Citizens' Committee to Protect Our Homes and Children was formed. The committee warned parents to vote against the amendment, saying the parents would be fined if they asked their kids to do chores around the house. "Who do you want to control your kids," the committee asked, "you or the government?" The amendment didn't pass.

But things did get better. By 1930, the number of ten- to fifteen-year-olds working dropped from 18% to 5%. And the number of kids in school rose from 50% to 70%.

Then came the depression of the 1930s. Millions of grownups were out of work. Child labor seemed even more ridiculous. In 1938 the Fair Labor Standards Act was passed. That was twenty years after Congress made its first try. This time the Supreme Court approved the law.

Whew. A long battle for some kind of national child labor law was won.

That's an explanation of the history of what's happened in this country in child labor. Finally, grownups ironed out their differences and took a strong stand to protect you.

Individual states have all passed their own regulations. If the state you live in has stricter laws, then they are the ones that you are regulated by. Laws are still being changed in some states.

California Today

In 1976 California passed a new law that gives stiff penalties for child labor law violations. Here are the standards in California. These are for twelve- to seventeen-year olds. No work between 10 p.m. and 5 a.m. on school days, or from 12:30 a.m. until 5 a.m. on weekends. No more than four hours of work on a school day. Kids under 16 can't do certain kinds of work. No operating autos or trucks as part of the job. No work in gasoline service stations allowed, as well as other dangerous job sites. You must have a work permit from your school authority to take a job, except for odd jobs.

During the first ten months of 1976, California employers were fined $153,950. Of these, 113 employers were fined between $1000 and $5000 each for allowing kids under 18 to work in dangerous situations. Another 276 employers had to pay $100 to $500 each for hiring kids under 18 to work in dangerous situations. Another 276 employers had to pay $100 to $500 each for hiring kids without the necessary permits from the school authorities.

Do you know what the standards are for the state you live in?

The Fight Is Not Over

There are still kids working under terrible conditions. Most of them work in the fields or on farms. They are the children of migrant workers. These families travel throughout the year to where crops need to be picked. The families are poor. Work isn't steady, and the children's help is needed.

It's estimated that about one-fourth of all farm workers are under 16 years old. That means there are tens of thousands of kids doing this work. It's legal for them to work in the fields at any age so long as it isn't during school hours. That's not enough federal protection for sure. Stooping in 100-degree heat for ten hours a day, working in fields that have been sprayed with dangerous insecticides is no way to spend out-of-school time for kids. Yet it is perfectly permissible according to the law.

The System Has Bugs

Time to take a look at all this information and see where you stand on all this. The laws today generally protect kids from horrible treatment that they once had to endure. Even though there is still work to be done, the situation has improved enormously.

But the protection you get also comes with limits. Money is important to most people. It's important to kids. And with restrictions on the kind and amount of work you can do, you are limited in the ways you can earn money.

Here's an example. By the time Michael was 12, he was thinking about becoming a veterinarian. He liked animals. He thought he was good with them. His parents encouraged him to think about it too. There was a veterinarian with an office a short bicycle ride from where Michael lived. So he went to the office and got to talk to the doctor. He told him he wanted to be a vet some day, that he was good with animals, and asked if there was some part-time work he could do for an hour or two after school or on Saturdays. The veterinarian was pretty impressed. And he did need someone to help keep the animal runs clean and help once in a while in other ways. Michael's parents felt good that he'd done this. Everything was going smoothly. He went back to the veterinarian's office to fill out some forms. That's when the whole plan blew up. Michael happened to be a tall kid, and it never occurred to the vet to ask his age. He couldn't work. He needed to be 14 in his state to get a work permit, and the veterinarian couldn't hire him without one. Michael didn't work. (He did go on to become a veterinarian, though.) The law was a real limit here. The grownups all agreed, both with each other and with Michael. But the law said nothing doing.

Not many people are interested in removing your protection. The fear of the horrible lives kids used to have is still strong.

Another bug in the system. Suppose you do get a job that is OK according to the law. And you sign a contract saying that you agree to work for so many hours for so much pay. And the person who hires you is counting on you to do that work. What if you change your mind? Where would that leave the employer? Remember, as a minor, you cannot be held to any contract you make.

Also, if you work, the money you earn really doesn't belong to you. Your parents have the right to that money. Should that be changed?

Is there a way to change some of these laws without making the situation like it used to be? Is there a need to do so?

A Few More Federal Rules

Social security is a national system that gives money to workers when they're too old to work, so that when they retire, they still get some money every month to help out. Every worker has a social security number. You have that number for life. It's long. Nine digits long. When you get a job you have to have a social security number. In many cases, your employer automatically deducts money from your paycheck each month to pay into the social security fund. You've got no choice about that. It's the law. Anyway, where did you think the government was going to get the money to pay you later?

Do you have a social security number now? There's no age requirement. Parents can even get them for their babies. That's because the number is used as your identification number in other situations. Banks usually require it to open accounts. Sometimes you need it to get a driver's permit. It's such an important number that some people have memorized theirs. All nine digits. Ask some grownups and see who knows their numbers.

You could get your own card now. It's free. Look in the white pages of the phone book under United States Government and then under Social Security Administration. If you call, you can get instructions about how to get your card with your own number on it.

There's another federal requirement if you've been working regularly. That's federal income tax. When workers earn money, they pay part of it in taxes to the government. That's one way the government keeps running. It's required by law. In many cases, as with social security, the money will be deducted from your paycheck. Everyone who earns over a certain amount has to file an income tax return. That amount changes from time to time. There are state income tax laws too. They are different from state to state.

When you file, it doesn't mean you'll have to pay taxes. It may be just the opposite. You may have had a job where your employer deducted money regularly and sent it to the federal government. You may be entitled to get that money back. But only if you file your income tax return.

Isn't Anything Simple?

Don't they make anything a little easier for kids? How about a little protection in that direction? You've got that too. If you want to work and can find jobs now and then for neighbors, you don't need a work permit or a social security number. "Permits are not needed for odd jobs in private homes," is the way California law for kids working puts it. You need to check with your state regulations. You can baby-sit. You can do yard work. You can do household chores. You just do the work and get paid. And then get on with being a kid.

Chapter 8

The TV Picture

By the time you graduate from high school, you will probably have spent more time watching TV than doing anything else except sleeping. And that also means that you will have spent more than twice as much time watching television as you have in school.

You will have seen 350,000 commercials. You will have seen 18,000 murders. As a matter of fact, by the time you entered kindergarten, you spent more hours watching TV than you'd need to spend to earn a college degree.

That's a lot of hours.

Putting Yourself on the TV Line

What kind of a TV watcher are you?

Draw a line like this on a piece of paper. Mark the middle of it.

└─────────────┴─────────────┘

Imagine two kids, one standing on each end of the line. They represent two different kinds of TV watchers.

The one on the left first. This kid really watches a lot of TV. When someone comes over to this kid's house to do something, this kid always has the same suggestion. How about catching a little TV? This kid has so many favorite programs that having two TV sets to watch at the same time would be real handy. This kind of kid has an I-Love-TV tee shirt. And wears it a lot.

The kid on the right is different. Just never seems to notice TV. Walks into the room where people are watching it and starts to talk as if there was nothing

else going on. Watches things once in a while, but usually drifts off to do something else. Has no favorite programs to watch regularly. TV just has no big appeal to this kid.

Imagine that each spot along the line represents a different amount of time that people watch TV. From left to right the time gets less and less. Draw yourself in where you think you belong on the line.

Make a prediction about where the other people in your family and your friends would put themselves on the line. Then check them out and see what you learn.

Television is big business. More statistics: about 97% of all households in the United States have one television set; just under half of all households have two or more sets. For about two-thirds of the American people, TV is their main source of information about the world. More Americans have televisions sets than have indoor plumbing. And the TV boom is not just an American addiction. In a power shortage in Buenos Aires, Argentina, the people voted to dim the street lights instead of cutting down on how much time they could watch TV.

97% of all U.S. households have a TV set.

Just under half of all U.S. households have two or more sets.

More Americans have television sets than have indoor plumbing.

Tuning In the Big Fuss

Television has become an important part of the big fuss that grownups make over kids. Maybe some of this fuss has been made in your house by your parents. But outside your family too, grownups have gotten themselves into several snags over how they think TV should be for kids.

These snags have grown into big arguments or disputes, as grownups call them. Here are the grownups who disagree: the people who make the TV shows; the people who pay to have the shows made for you; the people who are very upset about much of what you see on TV; the advertisers who hope you'll spend your money on their products; the government who makes the laws about all of TV.

First, the people who make the TV shows. There are different kinds of these people. There are the people you see on TV. There are the people who make the cartoons. Others write scripts for shows. Then there are those who do all the technical work. They all work hard to make shows that they hope you'll like to watch.

Next, the people who pay to have the shows made for you. They are the television broadcasters. They're the ones who make decisions about what programs you'll get to see. They're the ones who run the TV stations near you. They put programs on the air that you can watch on your TV.

Then there are the grownups who are very upset about much of kids' TV. And they've got a lot to say about it. One important group of these grownups is called Action for Children's Television (ACT). This organization got started in 1968 when a group of concerned parents met in someones's living room in Massachusetts to discuss children's TV. They've gotten really organized since then and have managed to change some of what bothers them about TV for kids. But not enough, they say. They're busily working all over the country. Other groups have gotten in on the arguments. There are local committees on children's television in many cities. PTA groups have gotten interested along with groups of pediatricians and eye doctors. There are organizations that send out information about what shows you should and shouldn't be allowed to watch because you are a kid.

Another group of grownups is the advertisers. They've got some information they want you kids to have. Information for you to think about enough so that you'll be inspired to spend your money. And advertisers see TV as a delivery service. TV delivers you right to the advertisers and no one even has to move. Pretty convenient.

The government. The Federal Communications Commission (FCC) licenses and regulates all channels in the United States. The commission is a committee of seven grownups. They are appointed by the President for seven years. They have to follow a law — the Communications Act of 1934. That law says that all stations have to show programs that are "in the public interest, convenience and necessity." That means that it's the people who watch TV who are to be served by the programs. In 1971, the FCC set up a Children's Bureau. So you know they're into this fuss about kids and TV.

This is some big fuss.

But First, Some Information

In order to understand the arguments, it helps to know a bit about TV.

There are two major kinds of broadcasting stations that you get on your TV, commercial and public. First, commercial broadcasting stations. They pay for the costs of putting programs on the air for you by selling commercial time to advertisers. Most of these stations are hooked up with one of the three major networks in the country — ABC, CBS, NBC. These three networks each own five stations and each has almost 200 other stations hooked up with it. People who run commercial broadcasting stations are in business to make money. And they do. They make their money by charging the advertisers for the attention of the audience. That's you. That's why they're careful when making decisions about what programs to show. They want to make sure they show programs that you'll like enough to watch again and again.

Public broadcasting works differently. Most of the public broadcasting stations are hooked up with PBS — the Public Broadcasting Service. On public broadcasting, there's no advertising about special products. The programs are made for the public interest. Some are paid for by the government. The Corporation for Public Broadcasting (CPB) manages that money. Some are paid for by donations from organizations of TV viewers. Sometimes companies pay for programs, but they don't tell you about their products. They do tell you that they have paid for this public service by announcing that they brought this program to you.

The grownups who are upset about TV for kids are upset with the commercial broadcasting stations, not with public broadcasting stations.

Then there's cable television. You may have a cable hookup that gives you more channels and makes your TV reception much better. It sends TV through an underground cable instead of through the air. Cable TV has an effect on what you get to see on TV, but it is not big enough right now to be a part of the argument.

The Television Test

Do you know which of the programs you watch are on commercial television stations and which are on public broadcasting stations? See if you can list three of each kind. Then check them out in your TV listings.

What about the collection of three-letter codes? All of these have been mentioned in the chapter so far. Check out which ones you know and don't know. For each, what do the letters stand for and what effect do they have on what you see on TV? Ready? In alphabetical order: ABC, ACT, CBS, CPB, FCC, NBC, and PBS.

Check your parents and see how their TV expertise is. You may have to talk with them about this later.

CPB? Chunky Peanut Butter?

Argument Number One: The Big Sell

You know about commercials. You can probably run a few through your head as clearly as if you were watching them right now on TV. (Maybe you are watching them right now on TV. Kids have been known to watch TV while doing all sorts of other things.)

It's hard to ignore commercials. According to the advertisers, you're not supposed to ignore them. In 1976 advertisers spent about $6.6 billion for advertising on TV. To rent some time for advertising during evening prime-time viewing costs the advertiser $50,000 for one minute. For that money, they have to make sure you don't ignore their commercials.

Where do you kids fit in? You spend money. And you watch a lot of television. So. . .if a company wants to encourage kids to buy a particular product, it seems like a good idea for that company to tell kids about that product on television. And they've found that it works.

Think about your own spending habits. Answer yes or no to these questions.

①

Have you ever wanted anything you've seen advertised on TV?

②

Have you ever bought anything you've seen advertised on TV?

③

Have you ever asked your parents to buy you something you've seen advertised on TV?

④

Do you think products you see advertised on TV could make you happier?

⑤

Did you ever think your parents were mean because they wouldn't buy you something you had seen advertised on TV?

⑥

Have you ever felt out-of-it with your friends because your parents wouldn't buy you something you had seen advertised on TV?

The more you answered with a yes, the more you probably have been influenced by TV advertising.

What's wrong with the big sell? How come grownups have gotten so concerned about this?

Parents began to notice that commercials were having an effect on their kids. They noticed this while shopping in the supermarket with their kids. First they noticed it on the aisle with all the breakfast cereals. Then on the aisle with the candy. And when they heard about advertisements on the aisle with the vitamins, it all came clear. Kids hear all that information, remember it, and believe it.

Hurray! say the advertisers. These kids know what they want and get their parents to buy it.

Those advertisers are no dummies. They know that kids like snacks. And that kids like sweets. So most of the commercials on children's programs are snacks to eat. Snacks with a lot of sugar in them. So TV advertisers spend a lot of money telling you about snacks with sugar that you'd just love to munch on.

Wait a minute, say the parents, as you fill up the shopping cart with sugary munchies, this is not so terrific as you may think. Eating a lot of sugar is not good. Kids need balanced diets. Your bodies are still growing and developing. You need to eat food rather than all this sugary stuff.

There you are again, being taken care of by two groups of grownups who just don't see a situation in the same way.

The parents organized. Had meetings. Complained to the advertisers. Complained to the broadcasters. Complained to the government.

Hey, the parents said to the advertisers. How come you don't show kids' commercials about good, tasty, and nutritious things to eat? How about showing kids snacking on juicy apples, crunchy carrots, noisy celery? Anything but that sugary stuff. Three-fourths of all the advertisements for kids sell food or drink. And a study found that only 11 of the 85 products showed in ads urged kids to eat food without sugar. Maybe if kids saw more healthy snacks advertised, they'd go get healthier snacks the next time they got a case of the hungries.

Listen, the advertisers said. We're interested in selling our products. We're not in the celery business. We're not in the business of teaching a course on nutrition in our commercials. We're selling our products. Kids like them. Besides, snacks won't kill them.

The parents tried the broadcasters. They just shrugged their shoulders. If it weren't for the advertisers, there would be no TV, they pointed out. And then what would the kids do? (What would you do?)

The parents went to the government. The Federal Trade Commission can stop any advertising that is false or misleading. But it doesn't look at all the ads on TV. There are no strong regulations for com-

82

mercials. The Commission will hear complaints, so concerned groups have the responsibility to make specific complaints heard.

This made the parents unhappy. Complaints take time and energy. But they kept working. They've had some influence too. Some decisions have been made due to the pressure of groups of concerned grownups.

One decision had to do with vitamin pills. Vitamins were being advertised just like candy. Well, they're not candy. Kids can be poisoned from too many vitamins. A four-year-old in Missouri ate a whole bottle of vitamins and spent two days in the hospital recovering. When the vitamin pill advertisers got the complaints about cases like this by the parents' groups, they removed all their ads from kids' shows. Now, there is a government regulation that makes it illegal for vitamin ads to be directed at kids.

Another decision had to do with the hosts of the shows or the main cartoon characters. Sometimes they would give the commercial messages. Not fair, the grownups complained, especially for little kids. They won't be able to separate the show from the commercials. So the National

Association of Broadcasters agreed not to do that. Hosts could now sell products on other shows, but not on their own shows. It was a start.

Other groups have gotten public service announcements on kids' TV. Usually they are 30- to 60-second messages that are fun to watch and give kids information about nutrition or about becoming a better consumer. They've gotten commercial broadcasting stations to pay for these and to show them during the times kids most often watch TV.

It's not just the food commercials that concern grownups. It's the commercials for toys and games too. And the advertisements are too loud. They're often louder than the program they cut into.

Well, say the advertisers, we've cut down on the amount of time we use for the ads. It used to be 16 minutes an hour. Now we average 9½ minutes an hour. We only use 7 minutes an hour on prime time. On Saturday morning kids' programs, we have no more than 12 minutes an hour.

Big deal, say the kid protectors. You can squeeze 10 to 20 messages in 9½ minutes. That's more messages than anyone needs, especially messages we don't like.

Advertisements are often louder than the programs they cut into.

Check out the time used for commercials. Next time you're watching TV, keep a watch with a second hand nearby. Keep track of the number of seconds used for all the commercials during the program and see how much time gets used in that way.

It's not an easy issue, and the differences haven't been resolved yet. After all, some of the advertisers are also parents. They care about what kids eat. But being an advertiser is what they do to earn the money to feed their families. Try to imagine how they might feel about this predicament. It's not always a clear-cut matter.

Where do you stand on all this? Here are some ways to help you think about that:

1 What do you think about commercials directed at kids on TV?

- They're fine; kids can decide what's best for them.
- There ought to be some rules for commercials.
- There shouldn't be any commercials on kids' TV.

2 Make a list of ten commercials that are on TV now that try to convince kids that they should buy a certain product (or get their parents to buy it.) Rate each according to this code:

- Urges kids to buy it so they'll be happier.
- Urges kids to buy it so they'll be healthier.
- Urges kids to buy it so they'll be like other kids.
- Other reasons.

3 What about other commercials that you see, not necessarily aimed at kids? They all have their own time slots. For each, make a prediction about the general time the product is advertised or the kind of program it interrupts (sports, action show, comedy, old movie, cartoon, etc.). Then check out your predictions.

- Toys
- Cereals
- Shampoo
- Beer
- Cars
- Laundry detergents
- Insurance

Argument Number Two: Will Violence Hurt You?

Violence is a big part of television. And causes a big part of the hassle between grownups about what kids see on television.

What's meant by violence on television? That's when there is either some threat of physical harm or there is actual physical harm shown.

Think of the cartoons on Saturday morning TV. Those characters have incredible experiences. Heads get blown off by cannons. They fall off cliffs. They get run over by trucks. Flattened by cars. Dropped from hooks in the sky. Bopped on their heads. Crushed by rocks. Rolled over by boulders. And sometimes all in less than five minutes.

Think of the evening shows. People get shot. People get beaten up. People get strangled. Sometimes they're the troublemakers, lawbreakers, general bad guys.

But often they're the heroes, the good guys. Check out who uses violence when you watch TV.

You learn something from everything you see. What do you learn from seeing violence? That's what's troubling many grownups.

The argument goes like this. You do learn from TV. And you do imitate what you see on TV. Ever hear people singing advertising jingles? Now why in the world, some grownups ask, would anyone want to fill kids' eyes full of violent acts? The United States Surgeon General reported that violence on television does have an effect on kids. That it encourages this kind of behavior from kids. That kids learn that violence is a way to solve problems.

Nonsense, say the people who produce these shows. Kids can see the difference between TV and the real world. Just because you see some kung fu on TV doesn't mean you're going to kick your brother next time you're having a disagreement.

Besides, violence is exciting. And an exciting program means a bigger audience. And a bigger audience makes advertisers happier. And the happier they are, the more money the broadcasters make. That's called a chain reaction.

How much is your weekly violence intake?

Make yourself a form like this and find out. Keep it near the TV so it will be handy to use. Everytime there's a situation that fits one of the categories, make a tally mark.

A Week of Violence

Murders
Gunfights
Fistfights
Violence used to solve a problem
Talking used to solve a problem

So there you are again. In the middle of a heated argument between grownups who are arguing about what's best for you again. Keep hoping that their argument doesn't get too violent.

Argument Number Three: Does TV Show Life As It Is?

This argument moves to the evening prime-viewing time, between 7:30 and 9:30. Lots of kids watch TV then. The programs are often adventure programs and comedy programs. They show people in an assortment of situations.

The question: What are these programs telling you kids about life and the way it really is?

Think about those situation shows that you watch on evening television. Not the game shows or variety shows, but the adventure and comedy programs. Answer these questions for yourself.

1. Do you think these programs show life as it really is?

2. Are the people in these programs just like people in real life?

3. Do you know people like them?

Here are the specifics about the two different sides of this picture.

Look carefully at these shows, concerned grownups say. Kids see situations on these programs that give outdated and incorrect messages about how men and women behave. In general you see more men than women. And on adventure programs, almost six times as many men as women. Men are shown having twice as many different occupations as women. Men are often shown to be able to do more. They support their families. They solve more problems. More than half of the mothers in our country work outside the home. Is this true of TV mothers?

Do you think the shows you watch in the evening give you these messages? Some TV research could help you find out. You'll need to make a form like this before one of the shows starts. You may want to make an extra one for your parents or sister or brother. That way you can compare and see if you both did "see" the same thing. Get a book or clipboard to lean on and a pencil with a decent point. Get comfortable and tune in.

You'll need to tally the characters as they appear. Once you make a tally mark for a character they don't get any other marks during that show even if they come in and out of the action.

Observation Form

Name of Show_____

Date_____Time_____Channel__

Number of Main Characters

Male   Old_____

          Young_____

Female Old_____

          Young_____

Number of Minor Characters

Male   Old_____

          Young_____

Female Old_____

          Young_____

Kind of work done

Male_____

Female_____

That's not all, say the concerned grown-ups. It's bad enough that the programs give these messages. The commercials are even worse.

Now maybe you pooh-pooh commercials as being dumb. Maybe you think they really don't matter very much and go get a drink of water when they come on. But you probably see enough of them for some of that information to sink in. And here's what's sinking in from commercials shown during those evening programs.

There are about equal numbers of men and women on the commercials. Women even have more speaking parts. They show how a detergent got the really filthy laundry clean. How the floor cleaner got the kitchen floor really shiny. How a frozen sauce made the spaghetti meal really delicious. Mostly they are women doing home chores.

And then when another voice comes on the air to give you the scientific or other specific information, it is usually a male voice. The advertisers feel that a male voice has more authority than a female voice and they use them in this way over 95% of the time.

On commercials, men get to work, play, eat, drive a car, be a doctor. Women get to do housework, cook, shop, care for kids or sick men, serve others. Of all the times women are shown on commercials, they only have jobs out in the world that they are paid for one out of three times.

The conclusion: On commercials, men are the authorities. Men work more, play more, and eat more. Women are most concerned about how they look, and what they do most is housework, shop, cook, and take care of others.

Many commercials show men as being stupid when doing household chores.

How about some research on commercials? You can do it the same way as you researched the programs. Here's a handy form to use.

```
┌─────────────────────────────────┐
│                                 │
│         Commercial              │
│      Observation Form           │
│   Name of show_____       │
│   _____       │
│                                 │
│   Date_____       │
│   Time_____       │
│   Channel_____       │
│   Product_____       │
│   Number of people              │
│        Male_____       │
│                                 │
│        Female_____       │
│                                 │
│   Voices of people not shown    │
│        Male_____       │
│                                 │
│        Female_____       │
│                                 │
│   What were people doing        │
│        Male_____       │
│   _____       │
│                                 │
│        Female_____       │
│   _____       │
│                                 │
└─────────────────────────────────┘
```

None of this is to say that the shows aren't entertaining. They have to be or they don't last very long. But it's another way to look at the entertainment you see.

Some grownups aren't concerned about this at all. They see nothing wrong with showing men and women the way they're being shown. Other grownups find this absolutely shocking and no way to give information about life to kids who will be grownups some day.

Changes get made on TV every year. New prime-time shows usually start each fall. Commercials are different. Think about the new additions which weren't on TV last year when you started back to school. Think about the programs and commercials which have been dropped. Are there any patterns to these changes?

There has been a lot of pressure brought on the TV industry by groups that have specific concerns. These groups feel that giving a public license to broadcast means that the stations have a responsiblilty to carefully make choices about how life gets presented both in programs and in commercials. And changes do get made because of these groups.

Ask your parents about what kinds of shows used to be on TV that don't appear now. Compare new shows with reruns of older shows to see changes for yourself. And try to imagine what kinds of shows might be on TV of the future.

Maybe you can size up how you feel about this issue.

Is the TV a Member of Your Family?

How does the TV get treated in your house? Does it have its own room? Do you like it better than your brother? Does it get much rest? Here are some questions to get you thinking about your family's TV habits.

① How do people in your family decide what to watch?

- Turn on the TV and see what's on.
- Check the daily listing and decide.
- Check a weekly listing and plan the week.
- Watch only certain favorite shows.

② How does TV get watched?

- The whole family watches together.
- The kids watch separately from the parents.
- It's different at different times.

③ What happens when a TV program is over?

- Someone gets up and turns the TV off.

- People usually sit and wait to see what's coming.
- Someone checks the TV listing.

④ Does your family talk during TV shows?

- Always
- Usually
- Sometimes
- Never

⑤ What about programs you've seen?

- You talk about them with your family.
- You talk about them with your friends.
- You usually don't talk about them with anyone.

Can You Imagine What Your Life Would Be Like Without TV?

Check with your parents and see if they always had a TV in their house when they were growing up. Did your grandparents? Try to find someone who didn't grow up with TV and see if you can find out how their lives were different. It may help to have some questions prepared. These may help.

What did you do at night after supper?
How did you find out about the news?
Did you ever see cartoons? Where?
What did you do on Saturday mornings?
What about rainy days when you couldn't go out and play?
How did TV change your life?

Who Controls the TV Tuner in Your House?

Are there rules for how much TV you watch? Or what you watch? Here is how different families deal with this issue.

1. No rules at all. Kids can watch whenever and whatever they like.

2. Kids get a total number of hours a day they can watch. No more is allowed.

3. No TV is allowed during certain hours, like mealtime, before school, after ten o'clock at night.

4. TV is only allowed on weekends.

5. Kids can watch only public broadcasting programs.

6. Kids have to look at the TV listing and check programs with their parents before tuning in.

7. TV is only for times when you can't be outside or have no chores to do. It's OK in bad weather, evenings when homework is done, times like that.

8. There is no TV in the house.

Are you clear about your family's rules? If not, it might be a good idea to bring it up and see if the whole family could agree on how the TV gets handled. Check with your friends. See what kinds of TV rules they live with.

91

Do You Need to Go on a TV Diet?

Is it possible, do you think, to watch too much TV? Eye doctors don't worry about it. They say TV puts less strain on your eyes than reading. But you shouldn't sit too close. The formula for a safe distance to put between you and the TV is to measure across your screen and sit at least five times that length away. Also don't watch in a completely dark room. Don't wear sunglasses when you watch. And don't put the TV where there will be glares or reflections from lights or windows.

But is watching TV stopping you from doing or exploring other things in life? What things, you ask? Well, if you're watching too much TV, you'll never find out. You might try an experiment. Take one entire weekend and decide not to watch any TV at all. Plan some other things to do. See what that feels like.

Is TV All Bad?

No. TV is not all bad. It's one of the most exciting inventions of this century. It's had more effect on our lives than most other inventions.

Can you imagine the TV of the future? How about being able to dial and ask for any movie or TV show that has been made to appear on your set whenever you wanted to see it? How about TV where you could interrupt and ask the person something? That way a public official or a person running for election could find out what people in the community really want. Or if you were sick, you could go to your class through the television. What about a channel where anyone in the community who wanted to share some feeling or idea could? Do these things exist now? How could you find out?

The more you know about what affects you, the better chance you have to exert some control in your life. How much TV you let into your life and what parts of TV you let into your life are pretty much up to you. What are you doing with this control?

Chapter 9

Hollywood Rates for Kids

Have you ever thought that you've made a big impression in Hollywood? Well, you have. People who make films have a lot to think about: actors, actresses, costumes, sets, camera people, and you. Every person who ever makes a film thinks long and hard about you.

Here's how. All films have ratings. There are four possible ratings a film can have. And there is a complicated way that films get these ratings. Some grownups have the full-time job of giving films ratings.

And the only reason all this goes on is because of kids. Once again, grownups are trying to protect you. What from, this time? From the evils of the world again. There are things that many grownups think young people shouldn't see. They've set up a rating system that makes it impossible for you to see certain movies and gives your parents information so they can decide which of the others they'll allow you to see.

What Are the Ratings?

Here are the four possible ratings films can have:

G – Suggested for general audiences, any age.

PG – All ages admitted; parental guidance suggested.

R – Persons under 17 not admitted unless accompanied by parent or adult guardian.

X – Persons under 17 not admitted.

How the Ratings Are Given

Here's how it works. Filmmakers want to make films that will be shown in movie theaters. They know that their films will have to be submitted to a special committee of the Motion Picture Association of America. That committee has seven members. It's the rating board that gives each film its rating.

The filmmakers may decide to submit the script before even making the movie. That's kind of like handing in a story for your teacher to grade. With a few differences. Filmmakers submit the scripts, along with the rating they think each film should get. If the committee doesn't agree, they'll make some recommendations about what needs to be changed or taken out so a film can get the asked-for rating. The filmmakers can make changes and hand their scripts in again.

Imagine handing in a story with the grade you think it deserves. And then if the teacher disagrees, you get the chance to make the improvements necessary and try for the grade you want. Does that ever happen?

Filmmakers don't have to submit their scripts. That's not required because the final rating decision is made on the final film.

If filmmakers think that the board's rating isn't a fair one, then they can appeal the decision. There's a different committee that does that. It's bigger, up to 25 members. The filmmaker writes a letter asking for an appeal hearing. This committee listens to both sides of the argument and then makes a decision.

Who Gives the Ratings?

The people on the committees have all worked with the film industry in some way. Maybe they made films. Maybe they ran theaters where films were shown. Maybe they wrote about films for newspapers or magazines. Also included are people who work professionally with children — psychologists or psychiatrists. These people bring a different point of view about what's not good for kids to see.

Other people sometimes get asked for opinions. A representative from the American Humane Association often has sat in on film reviews. That's happened when there's a question about whether a movie shows excessive cruelty or inhumane treatment to animals. Kids don't get all the protection in this world. Animals are entitled too.

Who Should Give the Ratings?

There are some people who think that the film industry shouldn't have anything to do with the ratings. How can they be fair, these people wonder? After all, they work for the film industry.

Other people say no, that's not so. The reason the Association does this is because it needs to be done. And the Association feels it's better to do it inside the industry rather than get the government involved in making laws.

Suppose it was set up with people who had nothing to do with the film industry? Who would these people be? Parents?

Teachers? Rabbis, ministers, or priests?
Old people? Younger adults? Children?
College students? Poor people? Rich
people? People who live in the country?
People who live in big cities?

It gets more complicated. Who would
choose these people? How long would
they do their job?

Maybe it could be done so all citizens
would serve for a period of time, like
jury duty.

Who would pay for it?

All this can make your head spin.

Here's an exercise for you. Suppose
you got the job of choosing seven
people you knew to decide,
according to the rating system,
which films kids in your area
could see. Write down the
names of seven possible people
who you think you'd go along
with. After you've got your list
made, keep reading.

Here are some ways to analyze
your choices. Sort your list
like this:

① Write **M** next to all males 21
years old or older.

② Write **F** next to all females 21
years old or older.

③ Write a small **m** next to all males
under the age of 21.

④ Write a small **f** next to all
females under the age of 21.

⑤ Circle any **M, F, m,** or **f** that is
a member of your family.

⑥ Put a check next to any that
are teachers or other people
who work in the schools.

⑦ Put two checks next to the names
of people from the religious
part of your community.

Now take a look. Who would
you trust with this job?

Some grownups look at the whole issue very differently. They've got something to say about the whole idea of ratings. They think that no one has a right to tell a filmmaker to change a film. That this is a denial of the filmmaker's freedom of expression. And freedom of expression is one of everyone's constitutional rights. Would someone tell an artist to change a color on a painting? Or tell an author to change the end of a story?

I just don't like the way this is looking like my grumpy Uncle Max. Change it to a nice landscape.

Some critics of the movie rating system say it's the same thing as asking an artist to change a work of art.

The people who support the film rating system say that's not the case. No film-maker has to change any part of any film. Any film can be made and shown to grownups under the rating system with an X rating. All the rating labels do is tell something about whether or not the film is one that's OK for kids to see.

Now, how do you feel about that argument? How do you feel about the fact that the rating system denies you the right to see certain movies? Doesn't that in some way restrict your freedom to ideas and information?

The Rating Code

How does a committee decide what rating to give a film anyway? To understand this, you need some more information. There are official codes they follow. Here's a shortened version of the official Association codes in use.

First there's a general statement. It says it's important to have free artistic expression. But that it should be in "close harmony" with our society. The motion picture industry chooses to regulate its own films in that way and not give the control over to the government.

Then there are three paragraphs about you. They state that your parents have the major responsibility to guide you, and that includes the movies you see. The motion picture industry feels they have the responsibility to give parents information to help them make decisions about the movies they will allow you to see. But they don't think information is enough. So the ratings have been added for all films shown in the United States.

Here's what each rating allows.

G

Films with G ratings are OK for people of all ages. Kids can understand them. Any sexual material is shown in a loving relationship. Any violence is shown as a force of law and order, not as a choice for solving problems. There's always a clear definition of right and wrong.

PG

These films differ from the G films in these ways. Kids can understand the big theme in the movie. But there can be other themes which are important to the film which younger kids might not understand. It is possible to refer to sex outside of loving relationships, as long as that isn't done for the main characters. More violence is allowed, but it still must follow the guidelines in the G films. And there is to be a clear treatment of right and wrong in the film.

R

A film with an R rating is based on an adult idea. The idea is one that kids might not understand. The limits on sex, violence, and right and wrong do not hold. But the films are to be stories of people and their individual lives and should not suggest that others should do the same.

X

These films treat sex, violence, crime, or profanity in ways that don't meet the limits in the other categories. Film makers can apply the X rating to any film they like.

Read the codes over carefully. Next time you are watching a program on TV, see what rating that program would get according to the codes. Try some adventure shows in the evening. Try some cartoons on Saturday morning. Do it with your parents or friends to compare opinions.

Another argument. How can this committee of seven people make decisions for millions of parents? It's impossible to make a decision that all parents would agree to. Some parents may think that the ratings are too strict. Some may think the opposite. Some may not care at all.

The rating system restricts parents' rights as well. Your parents have the right to control you. But they don't have the right to allow you to see an X rated movie even if they want you to. Or to let you go and see an R movie without them. That means the film industry has decided to take over a part of your parents' rights without necessarily asking them.

This brings it all home for you. Do you have to check with your parents before seeing a PG film? How does this work for your friends?

And the important issue. How do you feel about grownups taking care of you in this way? Does all this have an effect on your kidhood?

Chapter 10

The Weak Link

It's clear that kids are under the control of their parents in many ways. The law is very definite. Parents have to support, educate, and control their kids. Those are their rights and their responsibilities.

What about kids who don't have parents, who are orphaned? What about neglected kids, kids who are not taken care of well enough by their parents? What about abused kids who are cruelly treated by their parents? What kinds of protection do these kids get?

This has been a problem in our country since colonial times. It's still a problem today. A very serious problem for some kids and parents.

Back to Colonial Times

In colonial times there were three different ways needy children were cared for. One way was to be sent to live in a home as an apprentice. Nathan Knight was eight-and-a-half years old. He was an orphan. This was in 1676. He was apprenticed into the home of Henry Brookens for a period of twelve years and five months. During that time, Mr. Brookens would provide Nathan with a home and food and clothing. And Mr. Brookens would teach him how to become a mason. Nathan was to faithfully serve the Brookenses in return.

Today kids are put in foster homes. The arrangement is different, but the idea of having substitute parents for a period of time is the same.

A second way of providing care for kids was institutions which housed children who had no homes. The other method of protection was called outdoor relief, when parents were too poor to take care of their kids, but weren't neglectful or cruel. The family would receive money to support their children at home.

Day-care centers were set up in the late 1800s where kids of working parents could be cared for while their parents worked.

Things Were Different in the 1800s

In the 1800s there was a change in how grownups felt that abused or neglected kids should be cared for. Institutions were thought to be the best places for them. That got them away from uncaring parents. It was felt that kids could be raised to be good citizens in these institutions. Before 1800 there were eight such institutions for kids in the United States. But just between 1825 and 1850, ninety more were built.

Apprenticeships were used less and less. That was partly because there were more factories, so less people worked at home like Mr. Brookens, the mason. Besides the country had finally gotten rid of slavery. And being an apprentice was like being a servant, which was just too close to slavery. There were some foster home programs that did get started. Kids went to live there as kids, not as servants. Also day-care centers began to be set up. The first one of those was opened in 1854. Kids of working parents could be cared for there while their parents worked. More were formed, and by 1900 there were about 175 day-care centers.

So in different ways, grownups were working to protect kids who were in need of help. But not enough. There were still many kids who were abused and neglected, and there wasn't much protection for them. In the second half of the 1800s kids like this began to get more attention.

Here's the story of an abused and neglected boy who became a court case. This was in 1869. Samuel Fletcher, Jr. was blind. He lived with his father and his stepmother in Illinois. One winter they kept Samuel locked up in their cold, damp cellar for several days. He managed to escape and his parents were brought to trial. The court found them guilty and each parent had to pay a fine of $300. That was a serious fine. In those days $300 was really a lot of money. What the court said was that even though parents have control over their children, kids must have the protection of the law against being treated abusively.

This is another story of a mistreated child. This happened in 1874. Mary Ellen Wilson was an orphan. She lived with Mr. and Mrs. Connolly in New York City. Mary Ellen called Mrs. Connolly her mama. She was badly mistreated. She was beaten by her mama. She was never allowed to go out and play, except at night in her own yard. She had no friends. When Mr. and Mrs. Connolly went out, she was left locked in her bedroom.

A woman visited the Connollys' next-door neighbor. That neighbor told her visitor about Mary Ellen. This got the woman very upset. She went to several institutions to get help. She had no luck. Finally she went to see Mr. Bergh. He was a very humane man and was the head of the New York Society for the Prevention of Cruelty to Animals (SPCA). Mr. Bergh was horrified that there were laws to protect mistreated animals, but no laws to help a child who was being cruelly treated. He got the police to rescue Mary Ellen. She was at that time a sickly eight-year-old with cuts and bruises on her face. She had to tell her story in court. Mrs. Connolly was sentenced to prison for one year. Mary Ellen went to live in an institution.

Six months after that, in December, 1874, the Society for the Prevention of Cruelty to Children (SPCC) was formed. They worked to rescue abused or neglected children and see that parents were punished. The SPCC were given a lot of power. They were given the power of the police. They could go into a home where they suspected a child was being abused. And if the suspicions were true, they could arrest the parents and take the child to an institution.

There were many other children who were also being mistreated. These kids were not kids who were being reasonably punished by their parents for misbehaving. You may sometimes feel your parents punish you unfairly or too harshly. But these were kids who were brutally mistreated. They were severely beaten, deprived, or horribly neglected. Whether they had truly done something wrong to anger their parents isn't the issue. The issue was their parents' cruel abuse, abuse that could lead to permanent damage or death.

By 1900 institutions were getting crowded. There were orphans in them, neglected kids, battered kids, along with kids who had broken laws. There were no homes for these kids. There were no ways for their parents to get help to change instead of just being punished.

The White House Notices

In 1909 the first White House Conference on Children was held. It was supported by the President, paid for by the federal government, and organized by people who were concerned about kids.

Here's how it started. James West was an orphan from the age of six. From that time on, which was in 1878, he lived in institutions. Later he became a lawyer and worked in Washington. When James West was 36 years old, Theodore Roosevelt was President. James West suggested to the President that there be a national meeting about orphaned, destitute, and other deprived kids. The President agreed. On January 25, 1909, 200 people came to Washington and met.

Three years after that first White House Conference on Children, Congress formed the Children's Bureau. That was a big step. There already were about 250 organizations in the United States that were child welfare agencies. They were formed after the Society for the Prevention of Cruelty to Children in New York City. But when the federal government set up the Children's Bureau, it was like saying that child welfare was very, very important. Important enough for the federal government to make it a national concern.

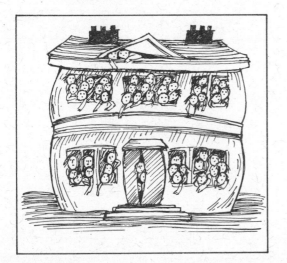

Child welfare became a concern that wasn't just for needy children. It was for all children. More grownups got interested in helping kids. The feeling was that wherever possible, kids were better off in homes than in institutions and child welfare agencies got involved helping kids in their homes. Lots more families adopted children.

The federal government stayed in on the act. There were White House Conferences on Children in 1919, 1930, 1940, 1950, and 1960. The themes of them changed from concerns about child health and welfare to things like learning to live in a democracy and learning to live full lives in a changing world.

The Problem Appears Again

But in the 1960s, the battered child came back into public view. Doctors and hospitals where abused children were treated helped inform the public. Newspapers carried more and more stories. The child welfare services weren't able to do all that was needed to be done.

Here's what happened to Roxanne Felumers. Roxanne lived with her mother and her stepfather. In 1969 she was badly enough abused by them to be placed in a foster home. But her mother missed her daughter. She got help from a social agency. The agency recommended to the court that Roxanne be returned to her own home. The court did this. Not long after that, Roxanne was killed by her stepfather.

This was a terrible tragedy.

The problem was a complicated one. Parents have a right to care for their children. Kids have a right to a loving home. The question is: When does the law step in?

For sure, if your parents punish you by hitting you for doing something they don't approve of, you're not going to get any protection from the law. As long as your parents are not endangering your safety, they have the legal right to punish you.

But Roxanne was dead.

And because of situations like hers, people began to think that keeping kids in their homes was not as important as keeping kids alive.

The problem is still a big one. About a million kids a year are mistreated by their parents. And about two thousand kids each year die because of this abuse. That's more than five kids a day. That's today in the United States.

A New Law Gets Passed

The federal government got worried about these statistics. A law was passed in 1974. It is called the Child Abuse Prevention and Treatment Act. One thing this act did was to set up a National Center on Child Abuse and Neglect with a plan to spend $85 million over a four-year period. So for sure, the concern has increased. The federal government has mostly worked to help local organizations tackle the problem in their own communities.

There are two needs. Protect the kids. Help the parents change.

About Parents Who Mistreat Their Kids

Who are these parents who abuse their kids? Why do they hurt their children? Many people have begun to study this more. Here's some of what they've learned. There is a pattern for when and how kids get abused or neglected.

First the parent. There has to be something in the parent's past that makes it possible for that parent to seriously mistreat his or her child. For most parents, this just isn't thinkable. And though no two abusive parents are exactly alike, there are some things they have in common. Most grew up in homes where there was a lot of violence. Violence was used when there were problems and that can become a habit. It's a nasty habit for sure.

Other patterns. These parents don't feel very good about themselves or what they do. They usually don't have lives that are very satisfying. They don't have enough helpful friends or families. Even though they may be near people, they feel very alone.

Of all the parents who do abuse their kids, 90% of them were abused when they were kids. Then they lived in fear of their parents' anger. Now they live in fear of their own anger.

Next, there has to be a kid. Sounds pretty obvious. But not just any kid. This kid is seen differently by the parents. The parents want the kid to grow up right. But the kid doesn't always do what the parents expect. And the parents either don't understand why the child is acting a certain way, or they don't know what's reasonable for kids to do.

Then there is some crisis. Something that pushes the parent into acting out against the child. The crisis makes the parent so miserable and hopeless, it triggers the possibility of hurting the child. Maybe the parent loses a job and has no money. Maybe the husband or wife left and the parent is terribly upset. Maybe a relative came to visit and is driving the parent up the wall. Maybe the washing machine broke and that was just one thing too much. And just at that time, the kid does something.

Parents who abuse their children live in fear of their own anger.

Parents don't have children so that they can beat them. But when that happens, both the parents and the kids need help. A great deal of help.

Sometimes the situation gets reported. By a neighbor. By a family member. By the parent maybe.

Who do these cases get reported to? Different agencies. Some are child protection services, juvenile or family courts, police or sheriff's departments, school systems, hospitals, doctors. Sometimes there are hotlines set up, phone numbers where someone can call at any time. Sometimes there are crisis centers for kids, where a parent can bring a kid they're afraid they're going to abuse.

Sometimes there are hotlines set up, phone numbers someone can call at anytime.

The Schools Can Help

Teachers are being trained to recognize abused and neglected kids and to be able to refer them for help. About half of all abused kids are school-aged.

Alan was in junior high. His physical education teacher noticed the heavy bruises and cuts on his back. He reported this to a social service agency. Alan told the child protection worker that he had been beaten. But he also said he thought he deserved it, that he was born bad anyway. He was actually protecting his parents, saying it was OK for them to beat him.

Jimmy was in the third grade. He came to school one day with black and blue marks on his face. His mother had hit him with a stick. She didn't mean to hit him in the face. But he ducked when she swung and got it. She felt Jimmy needed discipline because he was a bad boy.

Ann came to school with an ugly bruise on her cheek. She was seven. She said her father hit her. When the agency investigated, they found that wasn't what had happened. She had fallen. She admitted to that later and so did her sister.

Ann's mother had died a year before and her father worked long hours to support the kids. He didn't have much time with them. That night he had come home after the kids were asleep and they left for school in the morning before he saw them. The family did have a problem. Ann wasn't physically abused, but she didn't feel she was getting what she needed. Her lie was a way to give that information. She was being neglected.

What happens after a case is reported? First the kids. Sometimes kids get to stay at home and the family gets counselling. That's what happened in these three cases. Other times, the kids get placed in another home, where people are willing to make a temporary home for them. These people are called foster parents. Sometimes kids will go to a relative's house or to some kind of institutional home set up for kids. Or to the hospital; then the parents get taken to jail.

But the parents still need help. Some kind of counselling is needed to help them overcome their problem. And so do the kids. When you grow up mistreated and unloved, you need something extra to fill that space. Counselling can help.

Getting Help

How parents do get help varies. There have been efforts made to get parents in groups with other parents who have the same problem.

A mother started an organization in 1970. She had beaten her daughter and wanted help in order to stop doing this. And she wanted to help other parents with this problem. The organization is called Parents Anonymous. There are 150 chapters with about 1500 members in the United States and Canada. In 1974 the federal government's Children's Bureau gave that organization some money so they could help other parents form such groups.

Parents Anonymous tries to get as much publicity as possible, on TV, radio, in newspapers. Wherever possible. That's so there is some place for an abusive parent, or a parent who is afraid of being abusive, to go for help.

There is still much to be done. It's felt that kids should learn about these things in school. Not only about the atrocities, but also about parenting. About how to deal with things when they seem to be just too much. About what it takes to raise kids.

There was a class project in a school in North Dakota. Every student got the chance to see what it was like to be a parent. Each kid adopted an egg as their "child." Not a hard-boiled egg. A regular uncooked chicken's egg. And they had to take care of the egg for one week. If they wanted to do something or go somewhere without the egg, they had to find a babysitter or ask another "parent." No fair putting the egg in a safe drawer for a week. Remember Samuel Fletcher? His parents put him in a safe place — the cellar.

At the end of the week, most of the students felt that it was no fun having to take care of something all day long, every day. And eggs don't talk. Or need clothes. Or eat. Or want to buy a new skateboard. They just break easily.

You might want to try this and see how it feels to you. What does this have to do with abused kids? A cracked egg can't be put back together. All the king's horses and all the king's men had no luck with Humpty. Can abused children be put back together again?

Some grownups who work for the Foundation for Child Development in New York City think that the federal government should do a survey every year or two about kids. And that the people who get asked the questions ought to be kids who will give information about their feelings, how they live, what kind of care they get, and how they feel about their lives. Sound sensible? Maybe it will happen. What questions do you think they ought to ask? Try making up a questionnaire that you think would be helpful.

What About the Kids?

What can battered or neglected kids do? They need help from some grownup — a relative, a teacher, a school counselor, someone in a social welfare agency. These are people that any kid can go to who has a concern about child abuse.

But there are many abused or neglected kids who are under five years old. There's not much they can do to protect themselves or to get help.

Have you ever talked about this problem? With your parents? Teachers? Friends? It's one that everyone should be aware of. There are many, many kids who are in need of help. It's an unpleasant but serious problem and should not be ignored.

There's an old saying that says that a chain is only as strong as its weakest link. The welfare of kids today is not good enough until all kids get enough protection.

Chapter 11

Words Are Not Enough

People don't always say what they really feel or mean to say.
There are different reasons for this. Here are some examples. In
each example, someone is sending a message. And you are the
receiver. But there's a problem in each between what's sent and
what's received.

Sometimes people purposely don't say
what they feel. Maybe they don't want
to hurt your feelings. Let's say you spent
the entire day baking oatmeal almond
coconut cookies with chocolate chips and
raisins for a friend's birthday present.
You delivered them. Your friend looked
real pleased and bit into one. And chewed.
And chewed. And with a bit of coconut
sticking out between his two front teeth
said, "Wow, they're good. Really chewy.
Thanks." But somehow, something

about the way he said it made you think
that there's no career for you as the world's
best cookie baker.

Another example. Sometimes people
really don't know what they want to say.
Suppose you ask your parents for permission to spend the night at a friend's
house, a new friend and you're excited
that you got invited. And then you get
one of those fuzzy answers from your
parents. "We'll see." Or, "Maybe." Or,

"Check with me later." You don't know if that's a good sign or a bad sign. Usually it's OK with your parents to stay overnight. But maybe they want to check with your friend's family. Or maybe your grandmother might be visiting. Or something. You feel let down. You're wondering if it's worth it to try nagging a bit.

The third example. Sometimes people know what they want to say — but somehow when their words come out, you haven't gotten the message. This may happen in school when your teacher gives directions on how you're supposed to do a book report. You heard it all. It seemed to make sense. Everyone else has their heads down and their pencils scratching away on the paper. But you have no idea what to do.

Well, there are good reasons for these kinds of situations. There are experts who study how people communicate, what people really say to each other besides their words. It turns out that when you communicate with another person about some feelings you have, only 7% of the message is sent with your words alone. The tone of your voice accounts for 38% of the message. And your body language for 55%.

It's Up to You

If a situation comes up where you are the one left in an uncomfortable puff of words, it's up to you to do something about that. No protection is coming from grownups here. The control is all yours — not about what the other person said or didn't say, but what you decide to do about it.

There are three things that will help you in situations like these. One is to become a bit of a communications expert yourself. That means learning ways to "hear" what a person is saying not just with their words. That's what the experts mean about tone and body language.

Next is to see how you feel about the situation, not to shrug it off if it really matters. But also not to make a big deal, when that won't get anyone closer to understanding one another. And certainly not to do anything, unless you've got the other person's attention.

The third thing is to learn the knack of being as clear and direct as you can. That comes with learning about the first two things and a lot of practice. You'll get some ideas about how to do that.

A last note before you keep reading. Ever hear the expression "reading between the lines"? Do you know what that means? If not, ask someone. One of your parents can probably tell you. The whole idea of this chapter is learning how to communicate with people better, so you don't have to work so hard at reading between the lines.

Testing Your Tone

Tone first. That's pretty easy to learn about. For each situation described, you are going to ask, "Are you coming?" in a tone of voice that you think shows how you would feel. Say it out loud each time and try to listen to yourself.

SITUATION 1

You've agreed to take your little sister to the movies with you. She's putting on her shoes and taking forever to tie her laces. You're waiting outside with your friends! The movie starts soon. You call to your sister, "Are you coming?"

SITUATION 2

It's your birthday, and you've planned a pizza party for five of your friends. You've sent invitations. One friend hasn't answered. The party is in two days, and you want to know. So you call your friend and ask, "Are you coming?"

SITUATION 3

There is a craft show at the school on Saturday. There will be a rock band, food for sale. On Saturdays, your Dad usually relaxes at home. Besides, he hates rock music. But as you and your mother get ready to go, he gets up and puts his coat on too. You ask him, "Are you coming?"

Think of other situations where you could say it with still another tone of voice. Take something else to say, like "All right." Think of all the different tones you might use when you say that.

Here's another way to see how much your tone really does tell. Here's a sentence. Actually a question. "Did you give him that book?"

Now you get to say the sentence out loud six times. Each time you say it, put the emphasis on a different word. Ready?

1. **DID** you give him that book?
2. Did **YOU** give him that book?
3. Did you **GIVE** him that book?
4. Did you give **HIM** that book?
5. Did you give him **THAT** book?
6. Did you give him that **BOOK**?

Got the idea? Now go back over them one more time each. Imagine a situation where someone would ask the question in that particular tone of voice.

There are other languages in which the tone you use for the word actually changes the meaning of the word. Chinese is like that. There are four different tones you can give to each sound. And each tone gives the sound a different meaning. That makes Chinese a tonal language.

English is not a tonal language. *Give* means give no matter what tone of voice you use. But your tone does tell a lot about how you feel when you say something. Keep this in mind next time you're having a communication problem of some sort.

Tone might have been the clue to why you thought you'd never become a great cookie baker.

112

Your Body Language

Your body language tells more than half of what you are really "saying." That's what the communication experts think. Sometimes your body language says just the opposite of your words.

Have you ever had to apologize to someone when you really didn't mean it? Do you think the person you apologized to could tell you really didn't mean it? The clue might have been your body language.

Body language includes all the gestures you make with your body, your face, your hands or arms, the way you are standing.

Hands Can Talk

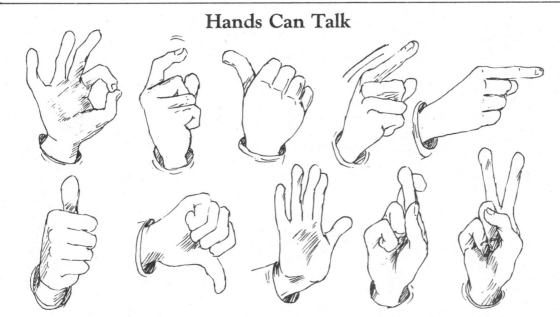

Do you know what each of these hand signs might mean? Here's an experiment to try. It's a good one to do with a friend or with your family. See how many hand signs you can think of that give exactly one message that you all agree on. No words allowed. And no facial looks to go along with them. Just your hands. Keep the game up until no one can think of any other sign.

The more you learn about gestures like these, the more you'll know about what people are feeling when they are talking to you. This can come in handy. Here are some things that the experts have found you can tell by watching people's hands.

1. They touch their faces. This may be by pinching their noses, rubbing behind their ears, rubbing their eyes with their fingers, touching their upper lips or the tips of their noses. These usually mean doubt, being unsure. Maybe one or both of your parents do this when you ask them for permission to do something, and they're not quite sure it's such a hot idea. Try it out and see.

2. They cross their arms. This often means some resistance to what you are saying. It's not necessarily negative, but they are not too open to the idea.

3. They drum or tap their fingers. This often means the person is bored. Their mind is wandering away from what you have to say. This is not a good time to ask an important question, but maybe not a bad time to ask a quickie question you're hoping to get a "yes" answer to.

4. They cover their eyes. Patience is wearing thin. Maybe the person is tired. Maybe the person is tired of you. Maybe you're being a first-class pest. Watch it.

5. They rub their hands. The person is usually looking forward to what you're suggesting. It's a show of expectation. A good sign.

6. They clap their hands. That's another good sign. It usually means approval. You've got the go-ahead.

A caution. Every time a person does one of these gestures with their hands, it doesn't necessarily mean what has been described. The gestures can't be separated from the situation. You need to check out your own observations. But once you learn a person's signals, they'll be pretty reliable for that person.

Another note. These gestures are unconscious gestures. That means a person doesn't think, "I'm bored; guess I'll drum my fingers on the table now." They drum on the table without first thinking it to themselves.

And a caution. Beware of itches. There is always the outside chance that the person just has an itch. That's why it's important to check out the gestures in more than one situation.

Your Face Tells Plenty

You can change your face into a lot of different positions. Some physiologists think that there are more than 20,000 of these different positions. Now, that's some pretty fancy muscle control. But actually only about 25 of those positions are expressions that the experts can describe.

Here's a game you can play with someone else to sharpen up your reading of faces. You need some index cards or small pieces of paper, ten for each of you. First of all, you both need to write the same words on your ten cards. Each word is a feeling. The sentences given after each feeling are to help you understand what feeling the word is describing. You don't have to copy the sentences. You can read them when you need them to help give you the feeling.

1. Happiness. (Oh, that's just what I wanted for my birthday.)
2. Surprise. (Wow, I didn't know you were coming.)
3. Fear. (Please don't tell my parents.)
4. Love. (I love my grandpa.)
5. Suffering. (I wish my toothache would go away.)

6. Disgust. (That brother of mine does such dumb things sometimes.)
7. Bewilderment. (I wonder how I'm supposed to do this problem.)
8. Anger. (You dropped my radio and broke it.)
9. Determination. (This time I'm going to get it right.)
10. Boredom. (I'm so bored I think I'll fall asleep.)

Here are the rules. The game is to be played silently. One player chooses a card from his or her stack and just with a facial expression tries to show the feeling on the card. This is where thinking about the sentences may help. The other player tries to find the matching card from the other stack. Take turns. Play the game until you both feel that you're terrific face readers. Also, try to see if there's more than one way to show feeling.

This is just practice. Try reading faces when you're outside with your friends. Or when you're in school. Or when you're eating supper with your family.

Smiles Talk Too

There are at least five different kinds of smiles that people can smile. And they each mean something different. Being able to read smiles can help you know more about what a person is really saying to you.

1. The Simple Smile. In this smile, no teeth show. It's kind of a quiet grin. Usually a person is smiling to himself or herself, and it's usually a show of contentment.

2. The Upper Smile. The top teeth show. This usually goes along with some eye contact. It's the smile that gets shown when one person is greeting another.

3. The Broad Smile. This is a big one. People do this when they're playing or laughing. There wouldn't be any eye-to-eye contact with this one. The person is too busy having a good time.

4. The Lip-In-Smile. The lower lip is a little bit inside the teeth in this smile. The upper teeth show. It's often a shy smile. The person you're smiling at may be a parent, a teacher, someone you feel is an authority in your life in some way.

5. The Oblong Smile. This is the fake smile. You see it in photographs sometimes. It's the smile you use when you're trying to laugh at a joke someone told you that you don't think is at all funny.

Cartoonists have these smiles down pat. They make cartoons and comics funny without words. Check the comics in the newspaper or any comics you have. Scan for smiles.

Try these smiles on in the mirror. Start checking out the smiles of the people around you. What kind of smile do grown-ups smile at you when they wish you'd find someone else to talk to?

A bit of history about the smile. It comes from the grin, and the grin was always a gesture of protection. The kind of expression you get when you grit your teeth and bare them at the same time. Animals use this gesture when they are being attacked, or when they want to scare off a possible attacker, or when they are taken by surprise and feel they might be in danger.

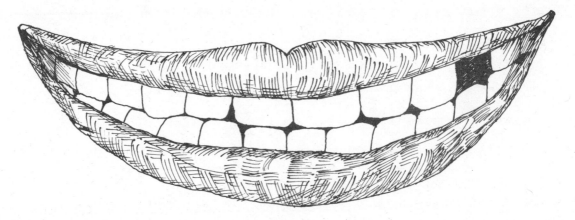

Imagine that a big box is about to fall on your head. And someone shouts, "Watch out!" Hunch up your shoulders and make a grimace with your face. Feel how your face muscles go. Not far from a grin.

OK, so how did the grin get from a sign of defense to an expression of pleasure? Well, think about when someone is walking toward you. Someone you don't really know, but someone who is going to greet you. The impulse is to smile. Smile number 2 to be exact. But when someone you don't know is greeting you, there is also a feeling of caution. You may even feel a little protective. It's something new. It's a combination of an open greeting and a bit of carefulness too.

Think about babies who like to play "Boo!" Each time they are surprised, they jump a bit and laugh and laugh. They want more. It's an expression of surprise and pleasure at the same time.

Most things that are funny have some surprise in them. The two just seem to go hand in hand.

Still More Body Talk

There are other things you do with your body that also talk. One thing is the distance you keep from other people. People you know well and care a lot about can come closer to you than strangers. When you're telling a friend a secret, you get real close. When you're just talking about not very important stuff, you stay farther away.

Try this experiment. Start talking to a friend about some usual thing. And as you're talking, inch closer and closer. Very slowly. There will be a distance which is a little too close for both of you. Your friend may start moving away or tell you to stop coming so close. You may feel it first, but don't react. You both have some private space that you don't always let other people into.

How about at the kitchen table? Is there a place that is yours? Do you ever have words with your brother or sister when they're crowding your space? And what tone of voice do you use then?

People nod their heads a lot. Really a lot. Try to talk and make an effort not to nod your head at all. See how that feels. One reason for the nod is so that the other person knows you're listening, that you haven't fallen fast asleep with your head up and your eyes wide open. Sometimes people nod when they're not really listening but want the other person to think that they are. Newscasters on TV don't nod very much. They've practiced this. Try watching the TV news with the sound off and observe their gestures.

Learning to understand nonverbal gestures is kind of like learning a foreign language, but everyone speaks this one. You may not have been aware of this, but it can help you when you're trying to communicate with other people. It can give you clues about how people around you are really feeling, no matter what they're saying with their words. It's another way to get a glimpse into the grown-up world that can be useful to you as a kid.

There is a difference between looking at people and really seeing them. Start seeing. It can make your life a lot more comfortable.

Presenting our hero, in a little story told with nonverbal gestures.

Words Do Count

Even though the ways you communicate without words are important, words do count. A lot. They may only transmit 7% of what you're feeling when you're giving some message, but you spend a lot of your time talking and listening to words. Here are some ways to look at how you and the people around you use words.

Who Do You Say Certain Things To?

People in your life fall into different categories. Some you don't know at all, strangers. Some you kind of know, but don't talk to about much of anything. These people are sometimes called acquaintances. Maybe they're kids in your class you're not very friendly with or friends of your parents who say "hi" when they come to visit. Then there are your friends. People you spend time with and talk to not because you have to, but because you like to. They can be kids your own age, or younger, or older. Even grownups. And then there are special people, the ones closest to you. People you care about a lot, and who you know love you too. Family. Friends.

Think of the people you know in a diagram like this. Where would you put each person in your family? Where would you put different friends?

When you use words to communicate, you say different kinds of things to each of these groups of people. For each of the things below, decide which category of people you would feel comfortable telling this to. Maybe to people in all of the categories. Maybe to just the one closest to you. Maybe just to yourself. It will give you another way to check out how you use words with the people in your life.

Who would you tell you get scared sometimes at night?

Who would you tell what foods you hate to eat?

Who would you tell how good you are at doing something?

Who would you tell how bad you are at doing something?

Who would you tell that you saw something that you don't think you were supposed to see?

You Know What I Mean?

Here's something people often say: "You know what I mean." Sometimes they say it like a question, "You know what I mean?" Sometimes they say it like a statement. Sometimes they say it a little differently, like: "You get it?"

Why do people say these things? Do they expect an answer? What do you do when someone says it to you? Nod? Shake your head no? Mumble something?

Try to pay attention and see if you're one of those people who says that a lot. It can become a habit that really adds nothing to your message. And if so, you might think about that.

Sometimes it's a way of finding out if the other person is receiving your message. Here's a suggestion. If you're not sure a person you're talking to is getting your message, ask clearly and directly, like this: "Are you understanding what I'm saying? I'm not sure if I'm making sense."

And if you're still not sure, ask the person what they think you are trying to say, like this: "Tell me what you think I mean. Then I'll know if I'm saying what I mean."

Don't leave the words up to both of your imaginations. That's like the situation when the teacher gave the directions for a book report and you never did get the idea.

Getting the Other Person's Attention

If you're going to say something that's important to you, no use wasting words. And if you're talking to someone who isn't listening, you're wasting your words. Not too good. You may think that grown-ups don't always give you complete attention. Think about that for a minute.

Suppose you want to get your mother to listen to you. You have something that is important to ask. You don't want to wait forever. What do you do? Try on these ways and see if any fit you. Each has its own problem.

1.

You just start talking. The problem: Halfway through the second sentence, your mother says, "Are you talking to me?" Then you have to start again. Wasting words, for sure.

2.

You stand very still in front of her until you're noticed. Then you start talking. The problem: This might take a while. A very long while.

3.

You tug on her or on part of her clothing. Wait for her to turn around and say "What is it?" Then you start talking. The problem: She might hit you.

4.

You raise your voice to get her attention. "Hey, Ma!" you might shout. When she says, "What?" you start talking. the problem: She might hit you.

5.

You go to a friend's house and call her up. When your mother answers the phone, you tell her what you wanted. The problem: She might start to yell at you for not being home yet. Then you're listening and not talking.

6.

You go outside and ring the front door bell and wait there until your mother answers the door. Then you tell her what you had in mind. The problem: She might be laughing too hard to listen.

There are always some problems with communicating. You've got to find ways to use words that make your problems as small as possible.

Here's another way for the attention problem that might work if all else fails. You write a note and hold it up in front of her. It says, "I'd like to ask you something sometime soon when you have a minute to listen. It's important." And then you wait patiently.

This one usually works. But don't overdo it.

A Fancy Word and What It Means

The fancy word: discretion. First you need to be able to pronounce it. The "e" is like the "e" in empty. And the accent is on the middle syllable. Got it?

Discretion is very important in trying to improve your talking skills with grownups. It's something you need to use when communicating with them. It's kind of like a bit of caution.

Here's an example. You need some extra money for a class field trip. You just heard your mother complaining about how expensive everything is getting and how she wonders where this will all end. Use your discretion. Don't ask now.

Or you finally really want an answer as to whether or not you can sleep at your friend's house. You start to nag a bit with maybe even a hint of a whine. Your father covers his eyes with his hand. That's hand gesture number 4, losing patience. Use your discretion. Ask later.

You can safely bet it would not be discreet to ask your Dad for a new bicycle at 5:00 a.m.

Discretion is a fancy word for being sensitive to other people and using your common sense. Practice it. When you do have something to say that can't wait, and your sense of discretion says it would be better to wait, good luck. One bit of advice: Watch that tone, that 38% of tone can make the difference. Wipe out those whines. This can work wonders.

There's More to What You Say Than What You Say

Read that sentence right above this one again. Then another time just to be sure. Communicating is one of the most complicated things you do. But it's also the way you get anything done with the people in your life.

Grownups take up a lot of space in your life. Paying attention to what they mean when they say something to you can reduce the amount of your hassles. A huge amount.

And what's most important is this. You are responsible for what you say. You have total control over that. It's one place in your life where grownups don't jump in to protect you. And they've probably given up teaching you what to say, except for a reminder now and then to say thank you.

Put some of your energy into saying what you really mean to say. You have a better chance of getting listened to that way.

Conclusion

One Last Look

Suppose you were given the job of planning the next White House Conference on Children. The President called you up and said, "I've heard that you're a pretty terrific kid. What I think this country needs is a White House Conference on Children that's been organized by pretty terrific kids. And you're one of those kids."

Suppose the President also said that one thing that's been said about all the conferences so far is that they were planned for grownups. Grownups who really were interested in doing more for kids and getting lots of other people doing more

for kids. And after seven conferences, they've run dry. So this time kids are going to plan the conference, so grownups can really get an idea about what's important to kids and what kids need.

Run this idea through your head a few times. What would be the theme? What would be one main thing you think a nationwide conference on kids should deal with? Who gets to come?

The big fuss grownups make about kids isn't getting any smaller. There's not much you can do about that, except learn more about how to live with it and then get on with living your own kidhood.